# THE CURIOUS
# COCKTAIL CABINET

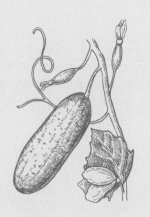

# THE CURIOUS COCKTAIL CABINET

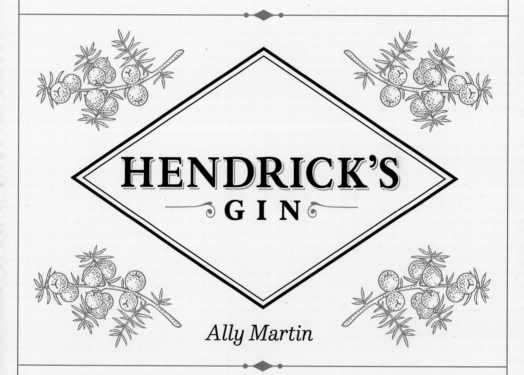

HENDRICK'S
GIN

*Ally Martin*

*100 recipes for remarkable gin cocktails*

ABRAMS IMAGE, NEW YORK

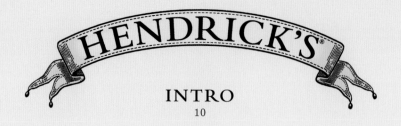

## HENDRICK'S®

### INTRO
10

### PART 1
•
## HISTORY, ELEMENTS
## & MATERIALS
14

PART 2
•
# COCKTAILS
40

PART 3
•
# DIY
218

# Hi, I'm Ally,

the Global Ambassador for Hendrick's Gin. I have the strange but amazing job of travelling the world enjoying incredible cocktails made by some of the most inventive bartenders out there. I'm also lucky enough to spend much of my working life behind the scenes of the gin world and dreaming up some curious cocktails of my own featuring Hendrick's Gin.

My obsession with cocktails began when I was a student, working in bars in Edinburgh, and to this day I still find it inspiring to see the unique and creative way that flavours come to life within a cocktail glass.

While I now travel all over the world with my job, I'm so proud to be Scottish and to represent a quintessentially Scottish gin. We're a small country but we've got this incredible reputation for knocking up great spirits. Getting to talk about my homeland and the great gins we make, in all corners of the globe, is a huge privilege.

Hendrick's Gin is a brand that has always done things in a different way. We are huge supporters of bartenders and I love to see what incredible new drinks they can mix with our gin.

This book is a collection of my favourite gin cocktails that I've either perfected over the years or had the pleasure of tasting. Each chapter also includes Hendrick's Gin cocktail recipes from some of the best bars in the world. Along the way I've included some of the stories and the inspirations behind these delicious drinks – it's not often you get to pull back the curtain and understand why your favourite cocktails are made in a certain way. Many of the bartenders I collaborated with on this book have also shared their secret sauces and homemade ingredients that add extra depth and character to the cocktails.

Within these pages you'll find curious twists on classic cocktails, summer stunners, drinks that make for tantalising toasts and sumptuous sharers – most of which you can prepare in advance and then serve up hot, cold or frozen, as the recipe suggests. As you delve deeper into the book, you'll discover cocktails that focus on specific unusual ingredients and limited libations for those of you who have snapped up some of our Cabinet of Curiosities limited releases and want to showcase them in a drink.

All in all, this is an eclectic mix of over 65 cocktails that highlight the versatility of gin, and Hendrick's Gin in particular. The recipes range from exceedingly easy serves for those taking their first steps in the world of cocktails to curiously complex creations for those wanting to flex their skills.

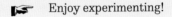     Enjoy experimenting!

# PART 1
·
# HISTORY, ELEMENTS & MATERIALS

# A potted history of Hendrick's Gin

HENDRICK'S GIN IS a refreshingly curious spirit made in a gloriously inefficient way in a little seaside town in Scotland on the rugged South Ayrshire coast. But how did Hendrick's come to be in the first place? Well, the two key people in Hendrick's history are Charles Gordon and Lesley Gracie.

Charles Gordon was the late-life president of William Grant & Sons, the independent, family-owned distillers that make Hendrick's Gin. Charles was a visionary who came from a long line of visionaries – many of whom have shaped the spirits world and created incredible whisky brands like Grant's, Glenfiddich and The Balvenie. Back in 1966, Charles acquired at auction the two unique stills that are used to make Hendrick's: an antique Bennett copper pot still dating back to 1860 and a rare Carterhead from 1948, of which only a handful exist today.

It wasn't until 1999, however, that he asked Lesley Gracie, who would become our master distiller, to embark on a quest to boldly create a gin 'unlike any other' – curiously at a time when gin had long since fallen out of fashion.

This gave Lesley the chance to combine her love of plants, fascination with flavour and formal chemistry training to develop the recipe for Hendrick's Gin using those two utterly dissimilar stills. Our two stills work in entirely different ways – the Bennett steeps our 11 botanicals in its base to produce a rich, deeply complex spirit, while the Carterhead steams the same dried botanicals in a basket above its lofty neck to create a light and fragrant spirit.

The results of these two distillations are then married together in a secret ratio to create a spirit that is delicate, yet full of depth. But even after all of that it is not quite yet Hendrick's. The coup de grâce is the addition of Bulgarian rose and *cucumis sativus*, commonly known as cucumber.

The first permanent addition to the Hendrick's Gin line-up beyond the original gin was Hendrick's Orbium, released in 2017. It was a very special quininated gin favoured by some of the very best bars in the world. Lesley wanted to combine Hendrick's Gin with some of the flavours she loved and push our liquid into an unexplored dimension using botanicals such as quinine (found in tonic), wormwood (found in Vermouth) and blue lotus blossom to create a complex gin with surprising brightness that makes for masterful martinis and other wonderful libations.

Almost 20 years after Hendrick's Gin was first conceived, we needed more space to make our curious spirits. So we finally built a suitably fitting home for the brand, the Hendrick's Gin Palace, which first opened its doors in 2018.

The Hendrick's Gin Palace is a sight to behold, if you're ever lucky enough to be invited to visit. Hidden beyond the walled garden you'll discover a Victorian-inspired palm house, flanked by two glass hothouses growing all manner of tropical and Mediterranean botanicals.

At the centre of it all lies our stillhouse, which contains the original Carterhead and Bennett stills, joined by some newer stills, which are exact replicas of those original two. Upstairs at the heart of the distillery are Lesley's Lab and her Cabinet of Curiosities, as well as the distillery bar where we test out new cocktails with Lesley's latest experiments.

With the Gin Palace up and running we were able to let Lesley's imagination roam free, release more limited-edition gins and share them with the world, each for a short period of time. Limited really does mean limited!

# Lesley's Lab

AT THE HEART of the Hendrick's Gin Palace is master distiller Lesley Gracie's lab, where she experiments with different botanical beauties and flavour combinations to create delightful liquids for our drinking pleasure.

Inside Lesley's lab is a flavour library hosting a huge number of distillates, essential oils, extracts and different botanicals that she's picked up on her travels over the years or created from botanicals grown in her beloved hothouses. Some have even been gifted to her by visitors from far afield.

Lesley's lab is also where you'll find the Cabinet of Curiosities, which is actually a real cabinet. All of her liquid creations are tucked up in here and every so often they are released to the world for a limited time. Each liquid is designed to evoke a different sensation based on a personal memory of Lesley's, whether it's the scent of flowers that bloom only under the light of the moon or soaking up the magic of the sea.

Over the past two decades she has been responsible for countless wonderful Hendrick's releases that have garnered immeasurable acclaim and recognition among the best bartenders in the world, as well as legions of spirits fans – like your good selves!

# WHAT IS GIN?

AT ITS SIMPLEST, gin is a juniper-based spirit produced by flavouring alcohol with botanicals of herbs, roots, spices and flowers, of which the predominant nose and taste must be of the wondrous juniper berry. There are three main styles of gin: a basic 'gin', 'distilled gin' and 'London gin'.

## GIN

To make a basic 'gin', flavourings – either natural or artificial – can simply be mixed with alcohol without having to redistill it, in a process called cold compounding.

## DISTILLED GIN

As the name suggests, a distilled gin is one that is made by distilling a neutral grain spirit in the presence of wondrous juniper berries. Hendrick's is a classic distilled gin.

## LONDON GIN

London Gin is a type of distilled gin, which, interestingly enough, does not need to be made in London. A key difference is that all of the flavour of a London Gin must be introduced exclusively through the redistillation of alcohol in the presence of botanicals, so no fancy flourishes of rose or cucumber afterwards. It can be called 'London Dry Gin' if minimal sweeteners have been added.

# OTHER STYLES OF GIN

### OLD TOM GIN

Original Old Tom Gin was a sweet liquid that is often described as the missing link between Dutch genever and modern Dry Gin. It had its heyday during the 1800s inside the Gin Palaces of London and was placed in barrels inside those very establishments, giving it a slightly darker colour. You won't find too many out there. Modern-style Old Tom Gins are still sweet but lighter and cleaner – as the quality of the base spirit has improved a whole lot since Victorian times.

### PLYMOUTH GIN

Strictly speaking, Plymouth Gin is not actually a different style of gin anymore; in fact, it never was. It is made in exactly the same way as most gins designated 'London Gin'. Since 1887, Plymouth Dry Gin could only be distilled within the city walls of Plymouth. The only company that made Plymouth Gin was Coates & Co, and in 2015 they announced that they were no longer seeking to protect the DOC status, effectively ending the category.

### SLOE GIN

Sloe Gin is a liqueur that is made by steeping sloe berries, the fruit of the blackthorn tree, in gin for several weeks and possibly adding sloe juice. The minimum alcoholic strength of sloe gin needs to be at least 25 percent and all flavourings must be natural.

# Essential equipment

SETTING UP A home bar doesn't need to be complicated or expensive. If you pick up just a few key pieces, you'll be blowing your friends' taste buds into next week in no time.

## SHAKER

If you only buy one piece of equipment for your home bar, get a shaker. There are all sorts of fancy ones out there but don't get flummoxed by it all. I prefer an all-metal one – perhaps because I'm clumsy and they're unsmashable. Either a two-piece or a three-piece shaker is perfect. However, there are other things you can use if you don't have one on hand – a jam jar or even some Tupperware will do a similar job if you shake it right.

## STRAINERS

When you shake a cocktail it creates lots of small shards of ice, so a strainer is a great way to get rid of these. There are a few different types of strainers out there, such as Hawthorne, julep and fine strainers. They each do a specific job and all are pretty handy to have around, but we'll walk you through that on p. 39.

## BARSPOON

These long spoons are perfect for two things: firstly, stirring a cocktail in a mixing glass and, secondly, well, all the things you'd normally use a spoon for. If you don't have a barspoon then something like a chopstick works really well, or anything else that's long and thin that you can find in your kitchen cupboard.

## JIGGER

A jigger is the perfect way to measure your cocktails with accuracy and make sure they turn out as delectable as possible. At home, you can easily get away with things like shot glasses or small measuring jugs. Even tablespoons (usually 15 ml) or teaspoons (5 ml) will do a nice job.

## MIXING GLASS

A mixing glass is a great addition, but if you're stuck then you can always use the tin of your cocktail shaker. You can get some really beautiful and elaborate mixing glasses but something simple will do exactly the same job. For example, if you find a jug that's not too big, that'll do nicely. You want something that will hold a good amount of ice but not too much, otherwise you'll drown your drink.

## KNIFE

You'll be cutting fruit for squeezing and preparing garnishes for your cocktails, so a good knife is really useful. Most small to medium sharp knives will work perfectly for all your cocktail escapades.

## CITRUS JUICER

Citrus is an important ingredient for many of the best-known gin cocktails and there are some great recipes in the upcoming pages that use citrus. The fresher the juice, the better the taste of your drink. A hinged juicer is probably best as it releases a lot of a fruit's fragrant oils into the juice.

## PEELER

For a wide array of drinks you'll need to create citrus peel garnishes. Peelers are perfect for this as they give you the great, zestiest parts of the fruit we're looking for without any of the more bitter, white pith that's hiding underneath.

# Gorgeous glassware

*Glassware is essential when it comes to making cocktails, for obvious reasons, but also because using the right glass for the right drink can be just as important.*

*If you can manage to pull together a small collection of quality glasses, you'll have everything you could possibly need to serve great drinks.*

## STYLING

### SHORT

Short means in a low glass like a rocks glass or an old fashioned glass. These don't have a stem and can be served with or without the ice, depending on the recipe.

### ON THE ROCKS

A drink served over ice in a rocks glass or old fashioned glass. Rocks in this context means ice cubes.

### UP

Up means in a glass with a stem, like a cocktail glass, flute, coupe or wine glass. Usually this will be without ice, but check the recipe.

### LONG

A long refreshing drink served in a tall glass with plenty of ice.

# GLASSES

## HIGHBALL

This tall glass is a magnificently versatile workhorse. It's essential for long and mixed drinks such as the Gin & Tonic and, of course, the highball. It's long and thin, meaning you can pack it full of ice, and its shape means it can maintain carbonation really well.

## ROCKS

These short and stout little glasses are also known as old fashioned glasses or tumblers. They're often used for drinks that are slightly on the boozier side, like a Negroni. Drinks served in these glasses are perfect with a big block of ice inside.

## COCKTAIL

Another one for the boozier little drinks. These stemmed glasses are small, fine and generally have replaced the classic V-shaped Martini glass because, well, they just look cooler.

## FLUTE

The most elegant of this ensemble of glassware, flutes are small and delicate with a long stem designed to keep your mitts away from the sides of the glass itself. They are perfect for Champagne as they hold bubbles really nicely. In the gin world they are the home of the French 75 cocktail, among others.

## COUPE OR COUPETTE

A particular shape of cocktail glass that can hold slightly more volume. This makes it perfect for shaken drinks. Its broad bowl and delicate stem also makes the drink much less likely to tip over the edges.

## NICK & NORA

Nick & Nora is an elegant stemmed glass curiously inspired by and named after the cocktail-loving characters in a classic detective film, *The Thin Man*. It's not an essential glass, but it is nice to have, as the tall walls mean guests are less likely to spill the contents than they are with a wide-rimmed cocktail glass.

## PONY GLASS OR SMALL-STEMMED SPIRITS GLASS

A pony glass is a short, stemmed glass about the size of a shot glass and is traditionally used for spirits and liqueurs – or teeny tiny cocktails.

## TEACUP

A teacup is not necessarily a traditional cocktail glass, but at Hendrick's we're not exactly traditional. Feel free to be a little imaginative with your drinking vessels – we often use teacups for our shared punch serves, and we use a teapot if we're really going to town! Be creative.

*Mixing masterfully*

WHEN IT COMES to making cocktails at home, there are a million and one techniques, but there are only six you really need to master in order to make most serves with ease: shaking, stirring, straining, combining, building and garnishing.

## SHAKING

Some of the best gin cocktails out there are shaken, from the Gimlet to the Vesper Martini.

Why shake and not stir? Well, shaking a cocktail does a few things. It chills and mixes the drink while also diluting and aerating it. Aeration means to add air, which helps to give the cocktails a delightful texture.

To start shaking, pour your cocktail ingredients into the smaller part of the shaker without ice. Now it's time to assemble your shaker. Put the top part over the bottom and create a seal (otherwise things will get messy very quickly). Be sure that you do not add any carbonated ingredients, such as soda water or Champagne, as they're likely to make your shaker explode.

Grab the top of the tin with one hand, pop your other hand over the bottom, then shake energetically back and forth for around fifteen seconds. When you're done, give it a light tap with your palm where the two ends of the shaker meet and open it up.

## STIRRING

The Martini is probably the most famous gin cocktail out there and to make a great one you'll need to learn how to stir.

Kick things off by adding your ingredients to the mixing glass or jug. Then add your ice and stir delicately with your barspoon. As you stir, the ice should smoothly brush the inside of the mixing glass. Be gentle, as this is all about control.

I always stir my drink for 30 rotations. Feel free to have a little taste as you go and when you think it's diluted to perfection and tasting delicious, then it's time to strain.

## COMBINING

Simply add the ingredients to the mixing glass or jug.

## STRAINING

Straining is about removing all the small fragments of ice that were created during shaking or stirring. Removing these makes for a better texture to the drink and a much more delicious cocktail-drinking experience. There are three types of strainer – Hawthorne, julep and fine – and you'll need one of each to conquer the full cocktail repertoire.

The Double Strain – Shaking a drink creates A LOT of cracked ice, and to get that velvety smooth cocktail experience you'll want to double-strain this out. That means using your Hawthorne strainer to remove the big pieces of ice and then pouring the cocktail through the fine strainer to remove the small pieces.

The Single Strain – You can single-strain using a Hawthorne or a julep strainer. It makes the most sense to single-strain a shaken drink if you're pouring it over crushed or cubed ice.

## BUILDING

Don't overlook built drinks. They might seem simple, but something like a Collins or a Gin Rickey can be the most satisfying of cocktail experiences. They're also a great place to start if you don't have a shaker on hand.

With built drinks, it's all about making sure the ingredients are balanced through the cocktail and that they have been combined perfectly.

Start off by adding your ice – lots of it, right to the brim. You want your cocktails to be cold. Then add your main ingredients and stir gently before adding some more ice and other ingredients like soda, tonic or Champagne. Then stir it again before adding some more ice and garnishing.

## GARNISHING

Garnishing is an important part of so many of the cocktails you'll find in this book. From citrus zests to mint sprigs, they provide aroma and act almost like a greeting as you bring a cocktail to your mouth. Don't be intimidated by garnishing your cocktails – even if they're a little rough and ready they'll still be doing the job. The garnish you'll come across most in this book is citrus peel, which is simple to create – just use a paring knife or a peeler to remove the outer skin of a citrus fruit of your choosing. Try to avoid getting too much of the white underside of the skin or pith, as this can be a little bitter. To zest it, all you need to do is squeeze it lightly over the drink to express the oils, then either drop it into your drink or discard it, depending on the recipe.

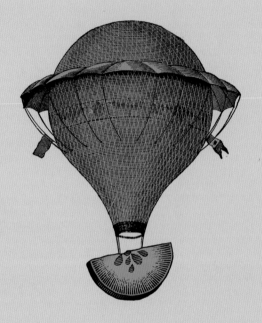

# PART 2

·

## COCKTAILS

EACH COCKTAIL IN this book has a key that will help you assess how quick and easy it is to make, what techniques you'll need to use and what glassware you'll need to have to hand. On p. 112 there's also a bunch of Sumptuous Sharers. At that point, we'll let you know how many servings each recipe makes, so feel free to multiply up and down depending on how many glorious guests you're entertaining.

☞ BUILT, SHAKEN OR STIRRED ☜

☞ GLASSWARE ☜

☞ SERVINGS ☜

# DIFFICULTY LEVEL

## EXCEEDINGLY EASY

———

A built drink or simply stirred serve that any beginner can throw together using ingredients you can find in your local store.

## ABSURDLY EFFORTLESS

———

A shaken or stirred and strained drink that will make you look like you really know what you're doing. Some of these have ingredients that are a little harder to find but they're worth the effort.

## INORDINATELY IMPRESSIVE
### *(yet somehow still surprisingly simple)*

———

A cocktail that requires just a little extra effort as you'll need to make some of the ingredients yourself – don't worry, we'll show you how.

## CURIOUSLY COMPLEX

———

For the real cocktail adventurers among you. These drinks take either a good amount of preparation in advance or a fair amount of concentration to prepare. But they'll be a real talking point at any party, and all taste delicious, so are completely worth all of that extra effort.

# Curious twists
# on classics

◆

*Classic cocktails have stood the test of time and are deliciously simple to whip up for friends. Here's a selection of my favourite classic gin cocktail recipes using Hendrick's Gin and a couple of curious twists on these much-loved tipples.*

*The classics continue to inspire the very best bartenders from around the world. It's always fascinating to see where they take these flavour combinations and how they reinvent them to make a thoroughly modern, exciting and delicious drink.*

•

◆

# THE CLASSIC HENDRICK'S & TONIC

| | |
|---|---|
| DIFFICULTY LEVEL | Exceedingly easy |
| MIXING METHOD | Built |
| STYLE | Long |
| GLASS | Highball |

### DESCRIPTION

*This really is the quintessential way to enjoy gin. It doesn't matter who you are, pretty much everyone has had a Gin & Tonic and it's usually their first experience of drinking gin. Sublime simplicity itself, this classic pairing with signature cucumber garnish highlights the refreshing complexity of Hendrick's Gin.*

## INGREDIENTS

- **1¾ ounces (50 ml)** Hendrick's Gin
- **4¼ ounces (125 ml)** tonic water
- *3 cucumber slices to garnish*

## DIRECTIONS

- Combine all the ingredients in a highball glass filled with ice and stir lightly.
- Garnish with three round slices of cucumber.

## CURIOUS FACT

During the 1800s, many British soldiers were stationed in India and other parts of South Asia, where they would struggle with outbreaks of malaria (and often scurvy). They were given tinctures made from quinine, an extract from the bark of the cinchona tree, to help with these ailments. But these concoctions tasted so awful that they began mixing them with their daily rations of gin to help the bitter medicine go down more smoothly and, in time, started adding sugar, water and lime into the mix as well. Hence, the Gin & Tonic was born.

# HENDRICK'S ORBIUM MARTINI

| | |
|---|---|
| DIFFICULTY LEVEL | Absurdly effortless |
| MIXING METHOD | Stirred |
| STYLE | Up |
| GLASS | Cocktail |

## DESCRIPTION

*The Martini, for me, is the king of cocktails. It has stood the test of time for a reason: it's simple, it's classy, it's delicious. The great thing about the Martini is that it's flexible and each person can flex it to their own liking. With so few ingredients it leaves nowhere to hide, and the quality of the ingredients, the proportions and the temperature are everything – the colder the better, in my opinion. This is my go-to Martini recipe that delivers every time. It's a 5:1, so five parts gin to one part vermouth, and it uses Hendrick's Orbium – a quininated gin based on the round house style of Hendrick's that makes for masterful Martinis. Lesley Gracie sees flavour in terms of shapes, and the Hendrick's style is round and smooth with no sharp flavours sticking out.*

## INGREDIENTS

- **1¾ ounces (50 ml)** Hendrick's Orbium Gin
- **⅓ ounce (10 ml)** Dolin Blanc Vermouth®
- Lemon zest
- *Cucumber slice to garnish*

## DIRECTIONS

- Pour all the ingredients into a mixing glass filled with ice and stir for around 20–30 seconds.
- Strain into a chilled cocktail glass.
- Twist the lemon zest over the glass to release the oils and then discard.
- Garnish with a cucumber slice.

## CURIOUS FACT

The base of Hendrick's Orbium is the Hendrick's Gin you know and love, but it's taken into another flavour dimension through the additions of quinine and wormwood – found in a G&T and a Martini – and blue lotus blossom, a sacred and spiritual flower in many parts of the world.

# ARUBEIBI MARTINI

| | |
|---|---|
| CREATED BY | Kevin Gómez, Aruba Day Drink Bar, Tijuana, Mexico |
| BAR | A bright spot to enjoy well-crafted cocktails in Mexico |
| DIFFICULTY LEVEL | Exceedingly easy |
| MIXING METHOD | Stirred |
| STYLE | Up |
| GLASS | Nick & Nora or cocktail glass |

## DESCRIPTION

*A floral twist on a Martini. This is a drink where keeping things simple really pays off. Let the quality of the ingredients shine through and balance each other beautifully.*

## INGREDIENTS

- **1 ounce (30 ml)** Hendrick's Orbium Gin
- **1 ounce (30 ml)** Carpano vermouth
- **½ ounce (15 ml)** St-Germain elderflower liqueur
- *A drop or two of olive oil to garnish*

## DIRECTIONS

- Add all the ingredients to a mixing glass with ice.
- Stir for about 20 seconds.
- Pour into a chilled glass with a stem.
- Garnish with a drop or two of olive oil.

# HENDRICK'S NEGRONI

| | |
|---:|:---|
| DIFFICULTY LEVEL | Exceedingly easy |
| MIXING METHOD | Stirred |
| STYLE | On the rocks |
| GLASS | Rocks |

### DESCRIPTION

*The Negroni is the classic aperitivo cocktail. Aperitivo is a tasty little Italian tradition of drinking certain cocktails before dinner to stimulate the appetite and get your taste buds going. For this recipe we keep it really simple and classic, using the traditional method of equal parts gin, Campari and vermouth, because if it's not broken, don't try to fix it.*

## INGREDIENTS

- **1 ounce (30 ml)** Hendrick's Gin
- **1 ounce (30 ml)** Campari
- **1 ounce (30 ml)** sweet vermouth
- *Orange twist to garnish*

## DIRECTIONS

- Pour all ingredients into a mixing glass filled with lots of ice.
- Stir for 10–15 seconds.
- Strain into a rocks glass over ice.
- Garnish with an orange twist.

## CURIOUS FACT

Aperitivo comes from the verb *aperire*, meaning to open, as in to open the palate or belly ahead of an upcoming feast.

# STRAWBERRY GIBSON

| | |
|---|---|
| CREATED BY | La'Mel Clarke, Seed Library, London, UK |
| BAR | A laid-back cocktail bar in the heart of Shoreditch focused on stripped-back analogue forms |
| DIFFICULTY LEVEL | Inordinately impressive (yet somehow still surprisingly simple) |
| MIXING METHOD | Stirred |
| STYLE | Up |
| GLASS | Nick & Nora |

### DESCRIPTION

*A Gibson is one of my absolute favourite cocktails, which is good because it's really easy to make. Simply garnish a gin Martini with a couple of cocktail onions or some other tangy treat to add a lovely little hint of savoury. This Strawberry Gibson is the perfect late-afternoon, middle-of-the-summer drink. It involves just enough prep to make you feel like you're a master bartender, but the recipe is easy enough to make while hosting an incredible gathering at the same time. It was inspired by the infamous addition of rose in Hendrick's Gin, the family of plants that strawberries come from. Something like the strawberry is really familiar on paper, but combine it with a little coconut vinegar and you will take this cocktail into a different dimension and surprise your taste buds.*

## INGREDIENTS

- 1¾ ounces (50 ml) Hendrick's Gin
- ⅔ ounce (20 ml) white vermouth
- ⅓ ounce (10 ml) strawberry and coconut vinegar (see p. 227)
- 1 pinch of salt
- *Half a strawberry for garnish*

## DIRECTIONS

- Add all the ingredients to a mixing glass and fill with lots of ice.
- Stir for 10–15 seconds.
- Strain into a chilled Nick & Nora glass (or any stemmed cocktail glass will do).
- Garnish with half a strawberry.

# LAST WORD

| | |
|---:|:---|
| CREATED BY | Marc Alvarez, Sips, Barcelona, Spain |
| BAR | An open-plan bar with a dark, moody atmosphere and incredibly inventive cocktails, which puts on a real show |
| DIFFICULTY LEVEL | Inordinately impressive (yet somehow still surprisingly simple) |
| MIXING METHOD | Shaken |
| STYLE | Up |
| GLASS | Coupe |

### DESCRIPTION

*This version of Last Word has two key variations: kumquat is added to the lime juice to give it even more mouthwatering acidity and aroma, and instead of the sweetness from cherry liqueur, a little naturally sweet muscat wine gives the drink a much rounder and more velvety touch. It's an inspired combination that adds freshness and texture to a well-loved classic and makes it a beautifully balanced, tangy drink.*

## INGREDIENTS

- **1 ounce (30 ml)** Hendrick's Gin
- **1 ounce (30 ml)** muscat wine
- **⅔ ounce (20 ml)** lime juice
- **⅓ ounce (10 ml)** green Chartreuse
- **⅓ ounce (10 ml)** yellow Chartreuse
- **1 barspoon** kumquat juice
- *Frozen kumquat slice to garnish*

## DIRECTIONS

- Combine the kumquat and lime juice to make klime juice.
- Pour all the ingredients into a shaker.
- Add ice to the top and shake.
- Place a big ice cube in a coupe glass.
- Fine-strain into the glass.
- Garnish with a slice of frozen kumquat.

## CURIOUS FACT

The Last Word is thought to have been popularised by Frank Fogarty, a famous theatre entertainer known for finishing his sets with a recital and so having the proverbial last word. This pre-Prohibition recipe was rediscovered and became a cult hit in Seattle in 2003 before it found its way onto cocktail menus around the world.

## TOP TIP

If you don't have a cocktail shaker or strainer, a jam jar will do the trick. Simply add all the ingredients, screw on the lid and shake. Slide the lid of the jar off a smidgen to allow the luxurious liquid to escape and hold back the ice.

# HENDRICK'S GIMLET

DIFFICULTY LEVEL    Absurdly effortless
MIXING METHOD    Shaken
STYLE    Up
GLASS    Coupette

### DESCRIPTION

*Aboard ships in the 1800s, scurvy was the scourge of all sailors, killing many due to a lack of vitamin-rich food available at sea. So in 1867 a product called Rose's Lime Cordial was created in Leith, Scotland: a concoction that combined fresh lime juice with sugar to preserve it. Royal Navy sailors were given a daily ration of the lime cordial and it wasn't long before officers were combining it with gin. In this recipe we've used fresh lime and a touch of simple syrup to balance out the drink and provide a touch of sweetness.*

### INGREDIENTS

- **1¾ ounces (50 ml)** Hendrick's Gin
- **¾ ounce (22.5 ml)** fresh lime juice
- **½ ounce (15 ml)** simple syrup (you can buy this from a shop or see p. 224 to make your own)
- *Slice of cucumber to garnish*

### DIRECTIONS

- Add all the ingredients to a shaker.
- Fill the shaker with ice and shake for 10–15 seconds.
- Fine-strain into a chilled coupette glass.
- Garnish with a slice of cucumber.

# GREEN BELT

| | |
|---:|:---|
| CREATED BY | Barney Toy, Clipper in Auckland, New Zealand |
| BAR | A sophisticated spot inspired by the magic of travel |
| DIFFICULTY LEVEL | Curiously complex |
| MIXING METHOD | Shaken |
| STYLE | Up |
| GLASS | Nick & Nora |

### DESCRIPTION

*This is a tropical spin on a classic gin Gimlet. Pineapple and green chilli are a great combination and make the fresh flavours of Hendrick's Gin really pop. This recipe is a little more complex, as it needs a few homemade ingredients to be prepared in advance, but that extra effort is definitely worth it.*

### INGREDIENTS

- **1 ounce (30 ml)** Hendrick's Gin
- **⅓ ounce (10 ml)** green chilli vodka (see p. 232)
- **1½ ounces (45 ml)** pineapple cordial (see p. 230)
- **⅔ ounce (20 ml)** lime juice
- *Drop of avocado oil to garnish*

### DIRECTIONS

- Combine all the ingredients in a shaker with ice.
- Shake for 10–15 seconds.
- Fine-strain into a chilled stemmed glass.
- Finish with a drop of avocado oil.

# GREEN TUXEDO

| | |
|---|---|
| CREATED BY | Giovanni Graziadei, Jigger & Pony, Singapore |
| BAR | A bar that creates fresh interpretations of the classics, the recipes that used to be listed in 'jiggers' and 'ponies', in a really warm and convivial environment |
| DIFFICULTY LEVEL | Absurdly effortless |
| MIXING METHOD | Stirred |
| STYLE | Up |
| GLASS | Pony glass or small-stemmed spirits glass |

## DESCRIPTION

*The Green Tuxedo is a brilliant and inventive twist on the Tuxedo cocktail. A Tuxedo cocktail has almost as many variations as a Martini and is similar in style. This cocktail is a celebration of the more vegetal notes of Hendrick's, using pear liqueur for a pop of sweetness and some pickle brine to push the savoury notes of the sherry and the cucumber character of Hendrick's Gin.*

INGREDIENTS

- 1⅓ **ounces (40 ml)** Hendrick's Gin
- ⅔ **ounce (20 ml)** Fino sherry
- 1 barspoon Merlet Crème de Poire
- ½ **tsp (2.5 ml)** pickle brine
- 1 dash of absinthe
- *Twist of lemon to garnish*

DIRECTIONS

- Add all the ingredients to a mixing glass and add some ice.
- Stir until combined and chilled.
- Pour into chilled pony glass.
- Garnish with a twist of lemon.

CURIOUS FACT

Jigger and pony is the name for a double-coned measuring device designed to accurately pour out spirits.

# MINT 500

| | |
|---|---|
| CREATED BY | Jason Scott, Bramble Bar & Lounge, Edinburgh, Scotland |
| BAR | An underground Edinburgh institution that operates with military precision to deliver tasty, creative offerings against a backdrop of good tunes |
| DIFFICULTY LEVEL | Absurdly effortless |
| MIXING METHOD | Shaken |
| STYLE | Up |
| GLASS | Cocktail |

## DESCRIPTION

*Created back in 2006, this drink has always been one that's flown off the shelf and into the glasses of visitors to this hip-hop-filled cocktail haven. There are a lot of great flavours in here, which create an incredibly fresh cocktail.*

## INGREDIENTS

- **1¾ ounces (50 ml)** Hendrick's Gin
- **⅓ ounce (10 ml)** pressed apple juice
- **½ ounce (15 ml)** freshly squeezed lime juice
- **½ tsp (2.5 ml)** vanilla syrup
- **½ tsp (2.5 ml)** elderflower cordial
- **6** mint leaves
- **2** basil leaves
- **1** dash of peach bitters
- **1** dash of egg white

## DIRECTIONS

- Pour all the ingredients into a shaker and 'dry' shake, which means to shake without ice.
- Then fill the shaker with cubed ice and shake rapidly.
- Fine-strain into a cocktail glass and garnish with a basil leaf.

# Summer stunners

*I love how refreshingly complex Hendrick's Gin is and how it can be mixed into delicious cocktails throughout the year. But during those balmy summer months it really comes into its own. Let's face it, who doesn't enjoy sipping on a delicious gin cocktail while the sun is shining? So, here it is, a compendium of some of my favourite summer serves to enjoy on long warm days when you're in holiday mode or simply want to bring a little liquid sunshine into your life.*

HENDRICK'S PEACH SOUTHSIDE

THE LESLEY GRACIE

WATERMELON CUCUMBER SPRITZ

KOMBU-CHACHACHA

THE STRANGWAYS

FRESH POST

JULY HULA

BREWBERRY YUM

SALTED BANANA MAR-TIKI

CROQUET CLUB COOLER

# HENDRICK'S PEACH SOUTHSIDE

DIFFICULTY LEVEL    Exceedingly easy
MIXING METHOD    Built
STYLE    Long
GLASS    Highball

---

### DESCRIPTION

*The Southside has a pretty convoluted history but it was developed in America long before Prohibition. It's a simple but refreshing drink that is served long and combines gin, mint, lime and sugar. We've taken this classic and given it a curious twist with the sweet surprise of peach liqueur (although if you don't have any, you can skip it and it will still be almost equally delicious). It's the perfect summer drink, with a sweet jolt and a gentle gilding of peach.*

---

### INGREDIENTS

- **1¾ ounces (50 ml)** Hendrick's Gin
- **¾ ounce (22.5 ml)** lime juice
- **½ ounce (15 ml)** simple syrup (see p. 224)
- Handful of mint leaves
- **½ tsp (2.5 ml)** peach liqueur
- *3 thinly sliced rounds of cucumber and mint sprig to garnish*

### DIRECTIONS

- Combine all the ingredients in a highball filled with crushed ice.
- Lightly stir.
- Garnish with three thinly sliced rounds of cucumber and mint.

### PRO TIPS

Smack the mint in your hands to release its oils and powerful aromatics before adding to this refreshingly herbaceous concoction.

# THE LESLEY GRACIE

| | |
|---|---|
| DIFFICULTY LEVEL | Exceedingly easy |
| MIXING METHOD | Built |
| STYLE | Long |
| GLASS | Highball |

### DESCRIPTION

*Hendrick's master distiller, Lesley Gracie, is obsessed with flowers and fills her garden and the distillery's greenhouses with as many as she possibly can. Of all the flowers, though, she loves the taste of elderflower the most, and it actually grows wild in Scotland. To satisfy her love for elderflower, I knocked up this delightful mix of Hendrick's Gin, elderflower cordial and soda water. Since then, it's all she seems to drink, so I named the drink in her honour. What's great about this cocktail is that it lets the gin shine and brings out its floral notes. If it's good enough for the revered palate of a master distiller, then it's got to be good, right? Give it a whirl and thank me later!*

INGREDIENTS

- **1¾ ounces (50 ml)** Hendrick's Gin
- **½ ounce (15 ml)** elderflower cordial
- **5 ounces (150 ml)** soda water
- *3 slices of cucumber to garnish*

DIRECTIONS

- Combine all the ingredients in a highball glass filled with cubed ice.
- Lightly stir and serve.
- Garnish with three thinly sliced rounds of cucumber.

# WATERMELON CUCUMBER SPRITZ

DIFFICULTY LEVEL    Exceedingly easy
MIXING METHOD    Built
STYLE    Long
GLASS    Highball

---

### DESCRIPTION

*A lusciously refreshing, fruity little number that is pretty in pink, bubbling with summer flavours and takes no time at all to create.*

---

INGREDIENTS

- **1 ounce (30 ml)** Hendrick's Gin
- **1 ounce (30 ml)** watermelon juice
- **1 ounce (30 ml)** Prosecco
- Soda water
- *Watermelon slice and cucumber slice to garnish*

DIRECTIONS

- Pour all the ingredients (except the soda water) into a highball glass with ice.
- Top with soda water.
- Garnish with a watermelon slice and a cucumber slice.

# KOMBU-CHACHACHA

CREATED BY · Ronnaporn Kanivichaporn, Mahaniyom Cocktail Bar, Bangkok, Thailand

BAR · Mahaniyom directly translates as 'very popular' and the bar creates 'resourceful' cocktails in which every part of the ingredient is used

DIFFICULTY LEVEL · Exceedingly easy

MIXING METHOD · Built

STYLE · Long

GLASS · Highball

### DESCRIPTION

*This recipe combines some of the best bits of the Gin Fizz, Pimm's Cup and Southside cocktails and mixes it with kombucha, a delicious fermented drink, with a refreshingly flavoursome result.*

## INGREDIENTS

- 1½ ounces (45 ml) Hendrick's Gin
- ½ ounce (15 ml) Pimm's No.1
- ⅓ ounce (10 ml) simple syrup (buy at a shop or see p. 224 to make your own in a snap)
- ⅔ ounce (20 ml) lemon juice
- 5–6 mint leaves
- 2 ounces (60 ml) sparkling kombucha
- *Lemon peel to garnish*

## DIRECTIONS

- Shake all the ingredients (except the kombucha) over ice.
- Pour over ice into a highball glass.
- Top with kombucha.
- Garnish with a lemon peel.

## PRO TIPS

Feel free to vary the amount of simple syrup depending on the sweetness of the kombucha that you use. You can also experiment with different varieties of kombuchas, as they will all give a different taste. For the adventurous among you, you could even start making your own kombucha.

# THE STRANGWAYS

| | |
|---|---|
| CREATED BY | Alessandro Palazzi, Dukes Bar, London, England |
| BAR | A London institution famous for its Martini trolley delivering some of the finest and stiffest Martinis in the world. The bar was a favourite haunt of James Bond author Sir Ian Fleming |
| DIFFICULTY LEVEL | Inordinately impressive (yet somehow still surprisingly simple) |
| MIXING METHOD | Shaken |
| STYLE | Up |
| GLASS | Martini or Coupe |

## DESCRIPTION

•

*Strangways is a character in James Bond's* Dr. No, *a spy based in Jamaica. This cocktail is light, floral and refreshing. It is something that could easily be enjoyed in the Jamaican heat or during summer anywhere in the world.*

## INGREDIENTS

- ¾ ounce (20 g) fresh cucumber
- ⅓ ounce (10 ml) fresh organic lemon juice
- 1¾ ounces (50 ml) Hendrick's Gin
- ⅓ ounce (10 ml) elderflower cordial
- 1 barspoon egg white
- *Slice of cucumber to garnish*

## DIRECTIONS

- Muddle (mash up) the cucumber and mix it with the lemon juice.
- Combine all the ingredients in a cocktail shaker and shake.
- Fine-strain into a frozen Martini or Coupe glass.
- Garnish with a slice of cucumber.

# FRESH POST

| | |
|---|---|
| CREATED BY | Meaghan Dorman, Raines Law Room, New York, USA |
| BAR | A very civilised speakeasy in Chelsea, Manhattan, if you can find it... |
| DIFFICULTY LEVEL | Absurdly effortless |
| MIXING METHOD | Shaken |
| STYLE | Long |
| GLASS | Highball |

## DESCRIPTION

*The gin highball is perfect for summer. It's low-effort, refreshing and there are endless variations for you to try. This recipe includes Suze, which adds a nice bit of vibrancy to this long, cooling drink that sings of summer. Great cocktails don't have to be complicated; often the best are the simplest.*

## INGREDIENTS

- 1½ ounces (45 ml) Hendrick's Gin
- ½ ounce (15 ml) Suze Aperitif
- ½ ounce (15 ml) simple syrup (see p. 224)
- 1 ounce (30 ml) lime juice
- 3 cucumber wheels in shaker
- Soda water
- *Cracked black pepper and a mint sprig to garnish*

## DIRECTIONS

- Add all the ingredients (except the soda water) to the cocktail shaker.
- Fill the shaker to the top with ice and shake for 10–15 seconds.
- Fine-strain into an ice-filled highball glass.
- Top with soda water.
- Garnish with cracked black pepper and a mint sprig.

# JULY HULA

| | |
|---|---|
| CREATED BY | Joshua Monaghan, Zapote Bar, Playa del Carmen, Mexico |
| BAR | Sensational service, bright flavours and a stunning lagoon location – a heavenly combination |
| DIFFICULTY LEVEL | Inordinately impressive (yet somehow still surprisingly simple) |
| MIXING METHOD | Shaken |
| STYLE | Long |
| GLASS | Coupe |

## DESCRIPTION

*The inclusion of sake here gives a really interesting depth and combines with the more peppery, sherbety notes of the celery syrup to create a bright, refreshing cocktail.*

## INGREDIENTS

- **1 ounce (30 ml)** Hendrick's Gin
- **1 ounce (30 ml)** Nami Sake
- **1 ounce (30 ml)** celery syrup (see p. 224)
- **1 ounce (30 ml)** lemon juice
- **2 ounces (60 ml)** chamomile tea
- **2 dashes** of orange bitters
- *Twist of orange to garnish*

## DIRECTIONS

- Add all the ingredients to a cocktail shaker.
- Shake over ice.
- Fine-strain into a chilled coupe glass.
- Garnish with a twist of orange.

# BREWBERRY YUM

| | |
|---|---|
| CREATED BY | Philip Stefanescu, Tropic City, Bangkok, Thailand |
| BAR | This bar packs a tropical punch. It's one of the best places to party and enjoy top-notch drinks |
| DIFFICULTY LEVEL | Exceedingly easy |
| MIXING METHOD | Shaken |
| STYLE | Long |
| GLASS | Highball |

## DESCRIPTION

*Philip Stefanescu hails from Sweden and wanted to create a drink that reminded him of those Swedish midsummers. The blueberry jam here works wonderfully when combined with Hendrick's Gin, mixed with mint and topped with the hoppy bitterness of the local beer. Do this and you've got one cool summer serve on your hands.*

### INGREDIENTS

- 1½ ounces (45 ml) Hendrick's Gin
- ¾ ounce (22.5 ml) lemon juice
- ¾ ounce (22.5 ml) blueberry jam
- ⅓ ounce (10 ml) simple syrup (see p. 224)
- 5 mint leaves
- 1 ounce (30 ml) lager
- *Blueberries and mint sprig to garnish*

### DIRECTIONS

- Shake all the ingredients (except the lager) in a cocktail shaker with ice.
- Strain into a highball filled with cubed ice, then top up with the lager.
- Garnish with a few blueberries and a sprig of mint.

# SALTED BANANA MAR-TIKI

| | |
|---|---|
| CREATED BY | Vance Henderson, Hendrick's Gin National USA Brand Ambassador |
| DIFFICULTY LEVEL | Absurdly effortless |
| MIXING METHOD | Stirred |
| STYLE | Up |
| GLASS | Coupe or stemmed glass |

## DESCRIPTION

*I'm not sure what is a more curious combination, salted banana or a tiki take on a Martini? Both are suitably intriguing and, added together, you have a tropical treat of a drink. Vance used his extraordinary imagination to create a drink that will instantly transport you to sunnier climes.*

## INGREDIENTS

- 1⅓ ounces (40 ml) Hendrick's Gin
- ⅓ ounce (10 ml) white vermouth
- 1 barspoon sweet vermouth
- 1 barspoon banana liqueur
- 1 dash of Angostura® aromatic bitters
- Tiny pinch of salt
- Lemon zest
- *Dehydrated banana chip to garnish*

## DIRECTIONS

- Combine all the ingredients in a mixing glass with ice.
- Stir very well for at least 30 seconds.
- Fine strain into a chilled coupe or stemmed glass.
- Twist a zest of lemon over the glass to release the oils and discard.
- Garnish with a dehydrated banana chip.

# CROQUET CLUB COOLER

| | |
|---|---|
| CREATED BY | Erik Lorincz, Kwānt London, England |
| BAR | Kwānt is Eric's first solo venture after many years as the celebrated Head Bartender at The Savoy, based in London's Mayfair, it serves all the spectacular drinks we know and love him for |
| DIFFICULTY LEVEL | Absurdly effortless |
| MIXING METHOD | Shaken |
| STYLE | Up |
| GLASS | Goblet or wine glass |

---

### DESCRIPTION

*A fragrant, floral drink with real depth of flavour and a burst of tangy tropical refreshment.*

---

### INGREDIENTS

- 1½ ounces (45 ml) Hendrick's Gin
- ⅓ ounce (10 ml) dry Fino sherry
- ½ ounce (15 ml) St-Germain elderflower liqueur
- 1 ounce (30 ml) fresh lemon juice
- 1 ounce (30 ml) fresh pineapple juice
- 2 tsps caster sugar
- *Strip of cucumber and any in-season fruit to garnish*

### DIRECTIONS

- Shake all the ingredients and strain into a goblet glass or wine glass over ice.
- Garnish with fruit in season and a strip of cucumber.

# Tantalising toasts

*This chapter is all about celebrations – when you get together with loved ones and want a little something special to mark the occasion. Hendrick's Gin is so well-rounded it can stretch in many different directions flavour-wise, making it perfect for any occasion. So, from brunch to after-dinner drinks, New Year's Eve extravaganzas to engagement parties, there is a Hendrick's Gin cocktail to make any event memorable.*

RED SNAPPER

SUPERSONIC GIN & TONIC

SHE SAID YES

HENDRICK'S FRENCH 75

FLOATING ROSE MAR-TIKI

GADFLY

CELERY SOUR

ATLANTIC DAISY

STOCKING FILLER

ARTEMISIUM ORBIUM

# RED SNAPPER

DIFFICULTY LEVEL    Exceedingly easy
MIXING METHOD    Shaken
STYLE    Long
GLASS    Highball

---

### DESCRIPTION

*The Red Snapper is essentially a Bloody Mary with a secret: it's made with gin. Hendrick's provides a really nice, vibrant character to this much-loved cocktail. Though famous as the star of brunch, the Bloody Mary may also be supped at later times of the day, because who doesn't like a little bit of savoury goodness?*

---

### INGREDIENTS

- **1¾ ounces (50 ml)** Hendrick's Gin
- **3⅓ ounces (100 ml)** tomato juice
- **½ ounce (15 ml)** fresh lemon juice
- 1 barspoon Worcestershire sauce
- 2 pinches of salt
- 1 pinch of celery salt
- 3 dashes of hot sauce
- *3 cucumber rounds and a lemon twist to garnish*

### DIRECTIONS

- Combine all the ingredients in a cocktail shaker over ice.
- Stir well and pour into a highball glass with ice.
- Garnish with three thinly sliced rounds of cucumber and a lemon twist.

### CURIOUS FACT

Worcestershire sauce is a fermented condiment made in the town of Worcester in the county of Worcestershire, England. It was invented by accident back in 1835 by the chemists Lea & Perrins. A local aristocrat had gone to them asking them to recreate an old recipe he'd tasted in Bengal, India. They duly recreated it for him but kept some aside for themselves to try. Although it was not really to their liking, they stored the concoction in their cellar. Sometime later they tasted it again and discovered it had completely changed in flavour inside the barrels, turning into the delicious sauce we know today.

# SUPERSONIC GIN & TONIC

DIFFICULTY LEVEL **Exceedingly easy**
MIXING METHOD **Built**
STYLE **Long**
GLASS **Highball**

---

### DESCRIPTION

*It's like a Hendrick's Gin & Tonic had a baby with an Espresso Martini.*
*A refreshing, long, coffee-fuelled cocktail with a cooling cucumber finish.*

---

## INGREDIENTS

- **1¾ ounces (50 ml)** Hendrick's Gin
- **1** barspoon simple syrup (see p. 224)
- **¾ ounce (22.5 ml)** fresh espresso (left to go cold)
- **3⅓ ounces (100 ml)** tonic water
- *3 thinly sliced rounds of cucumber to garnish*

## DIRECTIONS

- Combine all the ingredients in a highball filled with cubed ice.
- Lightly stir.
- Garnish with 3 thinly sliced rounds of cucumber.

# SHE SAID YES!

| | |
|---|---|
| CREATED BY | John Lermayer and Chris Hopkins, Sweet Liberty, Miami, USA |
| BAR | A Miami institution that lives up to its motto to 'pursue happiness'. Go there and you'll understand just what we mean. This serve is a true testament to one of the bar's founders and co-creators of this drink, the late John Lermayer |
| DIFFICULTY LEVEL | Exceedingly easy |
| MIXING METHOD | Built |
| STYLE | Long |
| GLASS | Highball glass or Julep Mug |

## DESCRIPTION

*She Said Yes! is a cocktail that could accompany any incredible event or simply an everyday celebration that spreads a little happiness. The combination of the bitter, the sweet, the dry and the bubbly provides a rounded sparkling drink to toast at almost any conceivable celebration.*

INGREDIENTS

- **1 ounce (30 ml)** Hendrick's Gin
- **1 ounce (30 ml)** dry sherry
- **¾ ounce (22.5 ml)** raspberry syrup
- **¾ ounce (22.5 ml)** lemon juice
- Club soda
- *Raspberries, mint and cucumber to garnish*

DIRECTIONS

- Churn all the ingredients (except the club soda) with ice in a highball glass or julep mug.
- Top with club soda.
- Garnish with raspberries, mint and cucumber.

# HENDRICK'S FRENCH 75

| | |
|---|---|
| DIFFICULTY LEVEL | Absurdly effortless |
| MIXING METHOD | Shaken |
| STYLE | Up |
| GLASS | Flute |

## DESCRIPTION

*This sophisticated synthesis of Hendrick's Gin, sugar, lemon juice and Champagne will start any soirée in sensational style and bring a certain sparkle to proceedings. In essence, this is a Tom Collins where the soda is replaced with Champagne. Now contemplate that for a moment. Yes, it is as delicious as it sounds.*

### INGREDIENTS

- **1 ounce (30 ml)** Hendrick's Gin
- **½ ounce (15 ml)** simple syrup (buy from a store or to make your own see p. 224)
- **½ ounce (15 ml)** lemon juice
- Champagne

### DIRECTIONS

- Add all the ingredients (except the Champagne) to a cocktail shaker.
- Add ice, shake well and fine-strain into a flute.
- Top with Champagne.

### CURIOUS FACT

The French 75 is traditionally imbibed on New Year's Eve. It was invented at Harry's New York Bar in Paris back in 1915 and is curiously named after a famously fearsome French gun – little wonder then that the Hendrick's French 75 hits with such remarkable precision.

# FLOATING ROSE MAR-TIKI

| | |
|---|---|
| CREATED BY | Vance Henderson, Hendrick's Gin USA National Brand Ambassador |
| DIFFICULTY LEVEL | Absurdly effortless |
| MIXING METHOD | Stirred |
| STYLE | Up |
| GLASS | Cocktail |

### DESCRIPTION

*This wonderfully elegant cocktail is simple to make and yet looks super impressive to your guests, who will definitely be wanting to take a picture of this one. It has a lovely fragrance from the rose and orange bitters and a gentle warming spice from the ginger and spiced rum that adds a delightful depth to Hendrick's Gin. The finishing touch is the rose petal garnish – an ode to the rose in each and every bottle of Hendrick's, which just sings of summer garden parties.*

## INGREDIENTS

- **1 ounce (30 ml)** Hendrick's Neptunia Gin
- **1 ounce (30 ml)** Sailor Jerry Spiced Rum
- **½ ounce (15 ml)** Lillet Rose®
- **½ ounce (15 ml)** ginger liqueur
- **2 dashes of** orange bitters
- Grapefruit peel
- *Rose petal to garnish*

## TOP TIP

Sometimes you want just a hint of the oils and aroma from the citrus peel for your drink but you don't want to include the citrus peel itself. Thankfully, you can still make great use of those old citrus peels by adding them to sugar, leaving them overnight and then using that sugar for your next basic simple syrup (see p. 224).

## DIRECTIONS

- Combine all the ingredients in a mixing glass with ice.
- Stir very well for 30 seconds or so.
- Fine-strain into a chilled cocktail glass and discard the grapefruit peel.
- Garnish with a floating rose petal.

# GADFLY

CREATED BY  Paul MacDonald, Friday Saturday
Sunday, Philadelphia, USA

BAR  A classy, upscale neighbourhood
joint in Rittenhouse, Philadelphia,
which serves up a short selection of
exquisite cocktails

DIFFICULTY LEVEL  Absurdly effortless

MIXING METHOD  Stirred

STYLE  Up

GLASS  Cocktail

## DESCRIPTION

*The Gadfly keeps it simple with four quality ingredients combined perfectly, with a devastatingly delicious effect. This is a floral, fragrant and complex twist on a Martini, with a gorgeous purple hue, that'll bring that little bit of elegance to your evening.*

## INGREDIENTS

- **1 ounce (30 ml)** Hendrick's Gin
- **1¼ ounces (37.5 ml)** Dolin Blanc Vermouth®
- **¾ ounce (22.5 ml)** Suze
- **½ tsp (3 ml)** crème de violette
- *Orange twist to garnish*

## DIRECTIONS

- Combine all the ingredients in a mixing glass.
- Fill the glass with ice and stir for 30 seconds.
- Strain into a chilled cocktail glass.
- Garnish with an orange twist.

# CELERY SOUR

| | |
|---|---|
| CREATED BY | Jason Scott, Bramble Bar & Lounge, Edinburgh, Scotland |
| BAR | An underground Edinburgh institution that operates with military precision to deliver tasty creative offerings against a backdrop of good tunes |
| DIFFICULTY LEVEL | Absurdly effortless |
| MIXING METHOD | Shaken |
| STYLE | Up |
| GLASS | Coupe |

## DESCRIPTION

*Adapted from an early 1900s non-alcoholic recipe, this delicious drink with a little tropical hint is an absolute delight, with a fresh green backbone and a velvety texture from the egg white.*

## INGREDIENTS

- 1¾ ounces (50 ml) Hendrick's Gin
- ¾ ounce (22.5 ml) fresh lemon juice
- ⅓ ounce (10 ml) pineapple juice
- ⅓ ounce (10 ml) simple syrup (see p. 224)
- 1 barspoon celery bitters
- Dash of pasteurised egg white
- *Strip of celery to garnish*

## DIRECTIONS

- Place all the ingredients into a shaker and 'dry' shake (shake without ice).
- Then fill with cubed ice and shake hard again.
- Double-strain into a coupe.
- Garnish with a thin strip of celery.

# ATLANTIC DAISY

CREATED BY Silver Lyan team, Washington, DC, USA

BAR A multi-award-winning bar from the Mr Lyan group – the first US outpost is rightfully winning all the plaudits

DIFFICULTY LEVEL Absurdly effortless

MIXING METHOD Shaken

STYLE Up

GLASS Nick & Nora

## DESCRIPTION

*Silver Lyan has a big focus on the exchange of ideas and to this drink they've brought in the influences of countries and cultures that explore coastal, cooling flavours. These bring out the bright, fresh elements of Hendrick's Gin and make it the perfect cooling drink for a hazy summer afternoon. The Manzanilla brings a salinity and bite that lifts the juniper.*

## INGREDIENTS

- **1½ ounces (45 ml)** Hendrick's Gin
- **⅓ ounce (10 ml)** lemon juice
- **⅓ ounce (10 ml)** simple syrup (see p. 224)
- **½ ounce (15 ml)** Manzanilla sherry (we love Lustau)
- **2 dashes** of Atlantic bitters (see p. 226)

## DIRECTIONS

- Shake all the ingredients together in a cocktail shaker with ice.
- Strain into a chilled Nick & Nora glass or stemmed glass.

## TOP TIP

You'll want to keep the drink as cold as possible, so chill your glass to prevent it warming up the drink.

# STOCKING FILLER

| | |
|---|---|
| CREATED BY | Duncan McRae, Former Global Ambassador for Hendrick's Gin |
| DIFFICULTY LEVEL | Exceedingly easy |
| MIXING METHOD | Shaken |
| STYLE | Up |
| GLASS | Flute |

### DESCRIPTION

*As juicy and delicious as the tangerine at the bottom of your Christmas stocking, this sparkling, citrus fruity number is bursting with flavour.*

## INGREDIENTS

- ⅔ ounce (20 ml) Hendrick's Gin
- ⅓ ounce (10 ml) Grand Marnier Cordon Rouge
- 1 barspoon fresh lemon juice
- ¾ ounce (22.5 ml) fresh tangerine juice
- Sparkling wine

## DIRECTIONS

- Combine all the ingredients in a cocktail shaker with ice (except the sparkling wine) and briskly shake over ice.
- Double-strain into a flute.
- Top up with sparkling wine.

# ARTEMISIUM ORBIUM

CREATED BY — Najade Bijl, Pulitzer's Bar,
Amsterdam, Netherlands

BAR — This bar on the banks of the canal oozes
effortless elegance and is inspired by
timeless classic cocktails

DIFFICULTY LEVEL — Curiously complex

MIXING METHOD — Shaken

STYLE — On the rocks

GLASS — Rocks

## DESCRIPTION

*A drink designed to honour the spirit at its heart – Hendrick's Orbium –
from the cucumber in the cordial to the rose petal garnish. The use
of absinthe in the cocktail is a great way to bring out some of the
wormwood and quinine, which are both botanicals used in Hendrick's
Orbium. This drink is inspired by both the French 75 and the Death in the
Afternoon cocktails, and it's a great aperitif: light and refreshing, with
a slight, pleasant bitterness that will whet the appetite.*

### INGREDIENTS

- 1⅓ ounces (40 ml) Hendrick's Orbium Gin
- ½ ounce (15 ml) homemade cucumber and white wine cordial (see p. 229)
- ⅓ ounce (10 ml) lime juice
- ½ tsp (2.5 ml) absinthe
- 1⅓ ounces (40 ml) soda water
- ⅓ ounce (10 ml) Brut Champagne
- *Rose petal to garnish*

### DIRECTIONS

- Shake the Hendrick's Orbium Gin, cordial, lime juice and absinthe in a cocktail shaker over ice for 10–15 seconds.
- Fine-strain into a rocks glass over a big ice cube.
- Top up with soda water and Champagne.
- Gently stir with a barspoon and add a rose petal to garnish.

### TOP TIP

For an expert finish, rest the rose petal on the ice cube.

# Sumptuous sharers

*Shared cocktails are a great idea. They are perfect for preparing in advance, so when your guests arrive you can give them your undivided attention. Also, there is something quite nice about everyone experiencing the same drink at the same time. You can be quite creative about your choice of drinking vessel, so the cocktail is picture perfect as well as delicious. Whether you're looking for a twist on a classic that can be easily batched or something creative and contemporary to share with friends – hot, cold or frozen – this chapter has you covered.*

WHITE NEGRONI

NOTHING COM-PEARS TO YOU

GREEN GIMLET

HENDRICK'S SUMMER PUNCH

HENDRICK'S ICED TEA

WEASEL PUNCH

FROZEY ROSEY

HOT SPICED APPLE

MR MICAWBER'S HOT GIN PUNCH

STORM IN A COFFEE CUP

# WHITE NEGRONI

| | |
|---:|:---|
| DIFFICULTY LEVEL | Exceedingly easy |
| MIXING METHOD | Batched |
| STYLE | On the rocks |
| GLASS | Rocks |

### DESCRIPTION

*This amazing alternative to the classic negroni was originally created by Wayne Colllins. It uses a lightly bitter French aperitif called Suze, which is made with gentian root. It's in the same ballpark as something like Campari but is a touch less bitter and a bit more green and earthy. It's a fantastic addition to this drink when combined with Hendrick's Gin and white vermouth. This version is batched up in advance so you can make your life much easier.*

## INGREDIENTS

### SERVES 6–8

- **6¾ ounces (200 ml)** Hendrick's Gin
- **6¾ ounces (200 ml)** white vermouth (I'd go for Dolin Blanc but there are plenty of options out there)
- **6¾ ounces (200 ml)** Suze
- **5 ounces (150 ml)** water
- *Orange twist to garnish*

## DIRECTIONS

- Grab yourself a clean, empty 3-cup (750 ml) glass bottle and use a funnel to add all the ingredients.
- Leave in your fridge to chill for at least 3 hours.
- To serve, shake well and pour into a chilled rocks glass filled with ice.
- Garnish with an orange twist.

# NOTHING COM-PEARS TO YOU

| | |
|---|---|
| CREATED BY | Tim Lefevre, Door 74, Amsterdam, Netherlands |
| BAR | A charming Prohibition-era-themed bar serving up a smart mix of creative and classic cocktails |
| DIFFICULTY LEVEL | Absurdly effortless |
| MIXING METHOD | Combined |
| STYLE | Up |
| GLASS | Nick & Nora |

## DESCRIPTION

*This drink is a twist on an old-school classic called the Tuxedo No. 2. In this case, the maraschino is switched up for some delicious pear liqueur, which works perfectly with Hendrick's Gin. The absinthe bumps up all the bright notes found in the gin and the aromatic sweetness of the white vermouth builds on the gorgeous floral character of Hendrick's. There are no crazy techniques required – what makes this drink is quality ingredients, good ice and nice glassware.*

## INGREDIENTS
### SERVES 6–8

- **9 ounces (270 ml)** Hendrick's Gin
- **9 ounces (270 ml)** Dolin Blanc
- **2 ounces (60 ml)** pear liqueur
- **12** dashes of orange bitters
- **6** dashes of absinthe
- **4¾ ounces (140 ml)** filtered water
- *Lemon zest to garnish*

## DIRECTIONS

- Grab yourself a clean, empty 3-cup (750 ml) glass bottle and use a funnel to add all the ingredients.
- Leave in your fridge to chill for at least 3 hours.
- To serve, shake well and pour into a chilled Nick & Nora glass or other stemmed glass.
- Garnish with a lemon zest.

# GREEN GIMLET

| | |
|---|---|
| CREATED BY | Paul Taylor, Your Only Friend, Washington, DC, USA |
| BAR | Essentially a party with sandwiches and cocktails. That's the vibe, what's not to like? |
| DIFFICULTY LEVEL | Inordinately impressive (yet somehow still surprisingly simple) |
| MIXING METHOD | Combined |
| STYLE | On the rocks |
| GLASS | Rocks |

## DESCRIPTION

*This is a great drink to batch in advance. Knock it out and store in a bottle or container in the fridge. When you're ready to drink it, simply pour and serve. It's tangy, refreshing and simple, yet has depth and complexity.*

## INGREDIENTS

### SERVES 4

- **4 ounces (120 ml)** Hendrick's Gin
- **3 ounces (90 ml)** salted lemon oleo (see p. 226)
- **1 ounce (30 ml)** green Chartreuse
- **1½ cups (350 ml)** cucumber water (see p. 223)
- *Slice of cucumber and sprig of mint to garnish*

## DIRECTIONS

- Combine all the ingredients in a tub, jug or glass bottle.
- Chill until very cold in the fridge.
- Pour into a chilled rocks glass filled with ice, or a teacup.
- Garnish with a slice of cucumber and a sprig of mint.

## CURIOUS FACT

An oleo saccharum or salted lemon oleo is a very old ingredient that has been used in making punches as far back as 1670 and pops up in some of the earliest cocktail books. Citrus peels are combined with sugar until the sugar begins to extract the rich flavours and oils locked inside. The result is a concentrated, fruity, tangy syrup which is perfect for a whole load of cocktails but works especially well in punches.

## TOP TIP

When preparing the cucumber water, strain the cucumber juice really well before combining with water.

# HENDRICK'S SUMMER PUNCH

CREATED BY · Charlie McCarthy
DIFFICULTY LEVEL · Exceedingly easy
MIXING METHOD · Combined
STYLE · On the rocks
GLASS · Teacup or coupette

## DESCRIPTION

*The joy of making punch is that it is a communal experience that can add a little theatre to a summer gathering among pals. There's something really nice about digging into a bowl of punch – it feels a little bit ritualistic. In this Summer Punch, Hendrick's Gin is the canvas upon which all other ingredients dance – crisp notes of apple, floral notes of elderflower and the freshness of citrus all combine with vibrant aromatics. A delightfully light and refreshing summer punch to be enjoyed at all warm-weather celebrations.*

## INGREDIENTS

SERVES 10

- **2 cups (500 ml)** Hendrick's Gin
- **6¾ ounces (200 ml)** lemon juice
- **3 ounces (90 ml)** elderflower cordial
- **1 ounce (30 ml)** Maraschino liqueur
- **4½ cups (1 L)** cloudy apple juice
- Summer fruits (strawberries, raspberries, cucumber and lemon wheels)
- *Cucumber wheels and a mint sprig to garnish*

## DIRECTIONS

- Combine all the liquid ingredients together in a large punch bowl or any other suitable vessel, a big flask or a teapot works perfectly well.
- Add plenty of summer fruits – think strawberries, raspberries, cucumber and lemon wheels.
- Add a handful of ice and serve in teacups over cubed ice, or in coupettes.
- Garnish with cucumber wheels and a mint sprig.

## TOP TIP

If entertaining a crowd, combine the ingredients in advance so you can quickly assemble drinks. Add ice when guests arrive to prevent over-dilution.

## CURIOUS FACT

The first recorded punch recipe dates as far back as 1638. According to historian David Wondrich, a German named Johan Albrecht de Mandelslo was producing 'a kind of drink consisting of aqua-vitae, rose water, juice of citroens and sugar' from his factory in Surat in western India.

# HENDRICK'S ICED TEA

| | |
|---|---|
| CREATED BY | Erik Andersson, Hendrick's USA East Coast Ambassador |
| DIFFICULTY LEVEL | Exceedingly easy |
| MIXING METHOD | Combined |
| STYLE | On the rocks |
| GLASS | Teacup |

## DESCRIPTION

*This is a really excellent summertime punch, especially for those roasting-hot days. Hendrick's Gin is mixed with black tea, which draws out its more aromatic notes, while rose and honey bring a floral sweetness, then lemon adds that zing. All come together in a punch that is perfect to enjoy over ice in a tall glass.*

## INGREDIENTS

### SERVES 4

- **6 ounces (180 ml)** Hendrick's Gin
- **2¾ ounces (80 ml)** lemon juice
- **⅔ ounce (20 ml)** rose liqueur
- **2 ounces (60 ml)** honey syrup
- **3 cups (720 ml)** black tea (chilled)
- *Orange zest or a slice of cucumber to garnish*

## DIRECTIONS

- Combine all the ingredients in a punch bowl with large ice cubes.
- Pour into a teacup filled with ice.
- Garnish with orange zest or a slice of cucumber.

## TOP TIP

Although many punches throughout history have put tea to good use, the first recipe of something closely resembling the Iced Tea was popularised at the 1904 World's Fair in St. Louis, Missouri, where the hot summer days sparked a trend for fairgoers to go in search of something to cool them down.

# WEASEL PUNCH

CREATED BY   Michele Heinrich, Yaldy Bar,
Frankfurt-am-Main, Germany

BAR   A beautiful bar known for its focus on
quality seasonal and local ingredients

DIFFICULTY LEVEL   Absurdly effortless

MIXING METHOD   Combined

STYLE   Up

GLASS   Coupe

---

### DESCRIPTION

*This punch, designed by the talented Michele Heinrich at Frankfurt's Yaldy
Bar, uses Assam tea as the lengthener, and the touch of peach liqueur gives
it a lush, fruity richness.*

---

## INGREDIENTS

### SERVES 8

- **1⅓ cups (320 ml) Hendrick's Gin**
- **⅔ cup (160 ml)** simple syrup (buy or
  to make your own, see p. 224)
- **⅔ cup (160 ml)** lemon juice
- **2¾ ounces (80 ml)** peach liqueur
  (we recommend Merlet Crème
  de Pêche)
- **1 cup (240 ml)** Assam tea (chilled)
- *Cucumber slices and mint sprigs
  as garnish*

## DIRECTIONS

- Combine all the ingredients in
  a punch bowl.
- Add large ice cubes just
  before serving.
- Ladle into coupes for individual
  servings with a cube of ice and
  garnish with a slice of cucumber
  and a sprig of mint.

# FROZEY ROSEY

CREATED BY   Vance Henderson, Hendrick's Gin,
USA National Brand Ambassador

DIFFICULTY LEVEL   Exceedingly easy

MIXING METHOD   Combined

STYLE   Frozen

GLASS   Wine glasses or tumblers

## DESCRIPTION

•

*Frozen cocktails are a lot of fun but they can also be seriously good, well-made craft cocktails in their own right. Here's a fun twist on a frosé – there's a little more bite here and a little more depth, but it'll still keep the party going long into the night.*

## INGREDIENTS

### SERVES 6

- **¾ cup (190 ml)** Hendrick's Orbium Gin
- **1½ ounces (45 ml)** absinthe
- **¾ cup (190 ml)** simple syrup (see p. 224)
- **3 cups (750 ml)** rosé wine
- **3¼ ounces (95 ml)** lime juice
- **1¼ tsps (6 ml)** Peychaud's Bitters
- *Dried rosebuds to garnish*

## DIRECTIONS

- Stir all the ingredients in a large jug with ice.
- Pour into wine glasses or tumblers to serve.
- Garnish with dried rosebuds.

# HOT SPICED APPLE

DIFFICULTY LEVEL    Exceedingly easy
MIXING METHOD    Combined
STYLE    Hot
GLASS    Teacup

---

### DESCRIPTION

*Hendrick's Hot Spiced Apple is a most peculiar yet perfect punch to greet friends in from the cold. It will grace guests with the festive flavours of Hendrick's Gin, spiced apple juice and heavenly hospitality.*

---

## INGREDIENTS
### SERVES 8–10

- **3 cups (750 ml)** apple juice
- **2** cloves
- **2** crushed cardamom pods
- **2** star anise pods
- **15–20** juniper berries
- Peel of **1** orange
- **3** dashes of orange bitters
- **⅓ ounce (10 ml)** simple syrup (see p. 224)
- **5 ounces (150 ml)** Hendrick's Gin
- *3 slices of apple and a pinch of nutmeg to garnish*

## DIRECTIONS

- Simmer the apple juice with the spices, juniper berries, orange peel, bitters and simple syrup in a pan for 15 minutes and transfer to a teapot.
- Pour the Hendrick's Gin into a teacup, then pour your spiced apple concoction over the top.
- Garnish with slices of apple, a dusting of nutmeg or serve with ginger biscuits.

## CURIOUS FACT

Juniper and orange peel are among the many fine botanicals found in Hendrick's Gin.

# MR MICAWBER'S HOT GIN PUNCH

| | |
|---:|:---|
| DIFFICULTY LEVEL | Exceedingly easy |
| MIXING METHOD | Combined |
| STYLE | Hot |
| GLASS | Teacup |

## DESCRIPTION

*This is a perfect drink to warm the cockles after a long day or to take in a flask out for a walk in the park on a chilly Sunday afternoon. Full of rich flavours, spice and aromatic sweetness, it's a great winter warmer and one I've pulled out at many Christmas parties over the years.*

## INGREDIENTS

SERVES 4–6

- **6¾ ounces (200 ml)** Hendrick's Gin
- **6¾ ounces (200 ml)** Madeira wine
- **2 tsps** brown sugar
- **6** large lemon and orange twists
- **1** small slice of orange
- **1** fresh pineapple (peeled and cored)
- **4 tsps (20 ml)** honey
- Juice of **2** lemons
- **3** cloves
- Pinch of nutmeg
- **1** barspoon cinnamon powder
- *Pineapple wedge and ginger biscuit to garnish*

## DIRECTIONS

- Combine all the ingredients in a saucepan and place on the heat.
- Let the concoction simmer for 20–30 minutes.
- Taste, adding lemon juice or honey depending on whether you prefer it sweet or sour.
- When it's ready, pour into a teapot and serve in teacups. Alternatively, serve in a traditional punch bowl.
- Garnish with a pineapple wedge and ginger biscuit.

## TOP TIP

This can be reheated, so you can make it ahead of time and warm it back up when you're ready to serve.

## CURIOUS FACT

Charles Dickens was a lover of punch and it crops up in many of his works. Even Bob Cratchit and Scrooge get in on the act. This punch, though, is inspired by Mr Wilkins Micawber, who is a character in *David Copperfield*. He was described as drinking 'a glass of punch with an air of great enjoyment'.

# STORM IN A COFFEE CUP

| | |
|---|---|
| CREATED BY | Susan Ann MacKenzie, Bar Garçon, Munich, Germany |
| BAR | Cocktails, artisanal coffees and light bites at a tiny, minimalist bar with outdoor seating |
| DIFFICULTY LEVEL | Absurdly effortless |
| MIXING METHOD | Combined |
| STYLE | Hot |
| GLASS | Coffee cup |

## DESCRIPTION

*This is a great after-dinner drink. It's the lean, fruity, cheeky sister of the classic Irish Coffee, made using Hendrick's Gin, cherry liqueur and coffee and finished with a fragrant dash of orange bitters and an absinthe float.*

## INGREDIENTS

### SERVES 1

- **1 ounce (30 ml)** Hendrick's Gin
- **⅔ ounce (20 ml)** cherry liqueur
- **2¾ ounces (80 ml)** freshly brewed filter coffee
- **1⅓ ounces (40 ml)** hot water
- **1 dash** of orange bitters
- **1 barspoon** absinthe blanche
- Orange peel

## DIRECTIONS

- Combine the Hendrick's Gin, cherry liqueur, coffee, hot water and orange bitters in a coffee cup.
- Float a barspoon of absinthe on top.
- Twist an orange peel over the cup and then discard.

### TOP TIP

For bigger gatherings, multiply the recipe and prebatch the gin, cherry liqueur, orange bitters and absinthe. Then just brew a big pot of coffee and combine quickly.

# Limited libations

*This collection of recipes uses our limited-release expressions of Hendrick's. At the heart of our distillery lies Lesley's Lab, where our master distiller works away creating endless new experimental elixirs, many of which end up inside our Cabinet of Curiosities.*

*text continues overleaf*

MIDSUMMER SOLSTICE SPRITZ

GYSPY FORTUNE

SOLSTICE SWING

MIDSUMMER LOVIN'

MOONLIGHT BUCK

ANGEL FACE MARTINI

NEPTUNE'S SECRET

FENNEL I APPLE

HENDRICK'S WILDGARDEN CUP

HENDRICK'S CLOVER CLUB

*The first creation to make it out of Lesley's Lab was Hendrick's Midsummer Solstice, in 2019, which was inspired by the way certain flowers react to the Midsummer Solstice, making them more delightful in flavour. Since then, Lesley has been inspired by the ephemeral light of the moon, the magic of the sea and flowers that attract precious pollinators. Each gin from her mystical cabinet is rooted in a rich sensorial memory and is designed to conjure up a fleeting feeling. There are plenty more exciting creations to come, but whatever emerges from the cabinet won't be around forever, so catch it while you can.*

*If you're lucky enough to have a bottle of any of these limited-release beauties in your home bar, here are a few choice recipes to experiment with and enjoy! If you've missed out, try the recipes with our classic Hendrick's Gin – they form the base of all of our limited-edition expressions, so they will work really well.*

# MIDSUMMER SOLSTICE SPRITZ

| | |
|---:|:---|
| DIFFICULTY LEVEL | Exceedingly easy |
| MIXING METHOD | Built |
| STYLE | Up |
| GLASS | Wine |

## DESCRIPTION

*Watch your cocktail blossom as Hendrick's Midsummer Solstice captures the essence of summer in every bubble. Share this summer cocktail recipe with your dearest friends and mix with the sun-dappled laze of an endless afternoon.*

## INGREDIENTS

- 1⅓ ounces (40 ml) Hendrick's Midsummer Solstice Gin
- 1 barspoon elderflower liqueur
- 1¾ ounces (50 ml) sparkling wine
- 5 ounces (150 ml) tonic water
- *Orange slice, cucumber slice and edible flowers to garnish*

## DIRECTIONS

- Combine Hendrick's Midsummer Solstice Gin, elderflower liqueur and sparkling wine in a wine glass over ice.
- Gently stir and top with tonic water.
- Garnish with an orange slice, a cucumber slice and an edible flower if you're feeling fancy.

## HENDRICK'S MIDSUMMER SOLSTICE
### RELEASED 2019

Hendrick's Midsummer Solstice was the first release from our Cabinet of Curiosities after we moved to the Hendrick's Gin Palace, where we had the space to create more lovely gin.

This cocktail is inspired by nature's true Summer Solstice, when the Earth is tilted maximally towards the sun, heightening the abundant aromas of flowers in full bloom. This especially unique gin is true to the Hendrick's original 'round' house style, but is infused with an array of essences that capture the aromatic intensity of a midsummer's day.

# GYPSY FORTUNE

| | |
|---|---|
| CREATED BY | Gina Barbachano, Hanky Panky, Mexico City, Mexico |
| BAR | A fantastic bar hidden away in a secret location that's worth finding |
| DIFFICULTY LEVEL | Absurdly effortless |
| MIXING METHOD | Shaken |
| STYLE | On the rocks |
| GLASS | Rocks |

### DESCRIPTION

*Inspired by the faith of those who visit fortune tellers, this fragrant, floral drink has a fresh green undertone and a little kick of heat that makes it super refreshing.*

## INGREDIENTS

- **1½ ounces (45 ml)** Hendrick's Midsummer Solstice
- **⅔ ounce (20 ml)** Italicus Rosolio di Bergamotto, an Italian rose liqueur
- **⅓ ounce (10 ml)** green Chartreuse
- 1 barspoon Ancho Reyes green chilli liqueur
- **½ ounce (15 ml)** lime juice
- 2 dashes of celery bitters
- *Coriander or edible flower to garnish*

## DIRECTIONS

- Combine all the ingredients in a shaker.
- Add ice and shake for 10–15 seconds.
- Strain into a rocks glass with ice.
- Garnish with a coriander flower or another edible flower.

# SOLSTICE SWING

| | |
|---|---|
| CREATED BY | Chloé Merz, Germany |
| DIFFICULTY LEVEL | Absurdly effortless |
| MIXING METHOD | Shaken |
| STYLE | Up |
| GLASS | Coupe |

## DESCRIPTION

*Nothing transports you to summertime faster than something sparkling and celebratory. This cocktail is a twist on the classic French 75, but with hints of tarragon and pastis to add some complexity. Both of those flavours go amazingly well with the signature cucumber notes in Hendrick's Gin, and bubbles go well with pretty much everything.*

## INGREDIENTS

- **1 ounce (30 ml)** Hendrick's Midsummer Solstice
- **½ ounce (15 ml)** fresh lemon juice
- **1** barspoon–**⅓ ounce (10 ml)** tarragon syrup (see p. 225)
- **1** barspoon Henri Bardouin pastis
- Champagne
- *Lemon zest to garnish*

## DIRECTIONS

- Add all the ingredients (except the Champagne) to a cocktail shaker.
- Shake with ice.
- Double-strain into a chilled coupe.
- Top with Champagne.
- Garnish with lemon zest.

### TOP TIP

Don't shake with the Champagne, as this will have explosive results.

# MIDSUMMER LOVIN'

| | |
|---|---|
| CREATED BY | Iain McPherson, Panda & Sons, Edinburgh, Scotland |
| BAR | A fun speakeasy-inspired bar offering great Scottish hospitality and deliciously creative cocktails since 2013 |
| DIFFICULTY LEVEL | Absurdly effortless |
| MIXING METHOD | Stirred |
| STYLE | Up |
| GLASS | Coupe |

### DESCRIPTION

*A fresh, fragrant, floral twist on a Martini. When you have ingredients this good, you don't need to overcomplicate things – let them sing!*

## INGREDIENTS

- **1¾ ounces (50 ml)** Hendrick's Midsummer Solstice
- **1 ounce (30 ml)** Muyu Jasmine Verte
- *Lemon zest to garnish*

## DIRECTIONS

- Stir the ingredients together over ice.
- Strain into a chilled coupe.
- Garnish with a lemon zest.

# MOONLIGHT BUCK

| | |
|---|---|
| DIFFICULTY LEVEL | Exceedingly easy |
| MIXING METHOD | Built |
| STYLE | Long |
| GLASS | Highball |

## DESCRIPTION

*A Moonlight Buck is a stunning sundowner, a stellar combination of Hendrick's Lunar Gin, ginger ale and lemon juice garnished with cucumber and a twist of lemon. Fresh, warming and simple.*

## INGREDIENTS

- **1¾ ounces (50 ml)** Hendrick's Lunar Gin
- **½ ounce (15 ml)** lemon juice
- Ginger ale
- *3 slices of cucumber and a twist of lemon to garnish*

## DIRECTIONS

- Combine gin and lemon juice in a highball glass filled with cubed ice and top with ginger ale.
- Lightly stir.
- Garnish with three thinly sliced rounds of cucumber and a twist of lemon.

## HENDRICK'S LUNAR GIN
### RELEASED 2020

Hendrick's Lunar Gin is inspired by the light of the moon. One evening, our master distiller, Lesley Gracie, was enjoying a Hendrick's in her garden. Our little corner of the world is part of what's called a Dark Sky region, which means the moon is very vivid and the stars shine more brightly because of a lack of light pollution. It makes clear night skies particularly inspirational. As the day turned to night, Lesley became transfixed by the unique aromas emerging from the garden. Some plants and flowers have a strong connection with the patterns of the moon, which makes them more intense under its light than they are during the day. It's those very botanicals that go into Hendrick's Lunar Gin, making it a refreshing gin with an alluring complexity and delightful warmth. It's best suited to being savoured as a sundowner or for night sipping, moon gazing and other sensible modes of contemplation.

# ANGEL FACE MARTINI

DIFFICULTY LEVEL    Absurdly effortless
MIXING METHOD    Stirred
STYLE    Up
GLASS    Coupette

## DESCRIPTION

*Hendrick's Lunar Gin makes some wonderful stirred drinks and works incredibly well with more aromatic ingredients, such as vermouths or flavours such as apple and apricot. This is brought to life in this Angel Face Martini, a small twist on a 1930s recipe by Harry Craddock.*

## INGREDIENTS

- **1⅓ ounces (40 ml)** Hendrick's Lunar Gin
- **1 ounce (30 ml)** Calvados or apple brandy
- **1 ounce (30 ml)** apricot liqueur
- *Twist of orange to garnish*

## DIRECTIONS

- Stir all the ingredients over ice cubes in a mixing glass.
- Strain into a chilled coupette or cocktail glass.
- Garnish with a twist of orange.

# NEPTUNE'S SECRET

CREATED BY  Jono van Lamoen, Ultramarijn,
The Hague, Netherlands

BAR  A steampunk-themed nautical bar

DIFFICULTY LEVEL  Curiously complex

MIXING METHOD  Shaken

STYLE  Up

GLASS  Coupe

---

### DESCRIPTION

*This drink pays homage to the landlocked secret lover of Neptune, the god of the sea, by combining the flavours of both land and sea to create the perfect love story in liquid form. Beetroot has this really earthy character to it, which is perfect for this complex sour drink.*

---

INGREDIENTS

- **2 ounces (60 ml)** Hendrick's Neptunia Gin
- **1 ounce (30 ml)** lime juice
- **⅓ ounce (10 ml)** beetroot syrup (see p. 224)
- **⅓ ounce (10 ml)** aquafaba (you can also use egg white)
- Pinch of pink pepper
- *Edible flower to garnish*

DIRECTIONS

- Combine all the ingredients in a shaker and 'dry' shake (without ice) for 10 seconds.
- Then add ice to the shaker and shake vigorously for 10–15 seconds.
- Fine-strain the contents of the shaker into your chilled coupe.
- Garnish with an edible flower.

### HENDRICK'S NEPTUNIA GIN
### RELEASED 2022

Hendrick's is located right on the Ayrshire coast with views out to the mysterious and magnificent Ailsa Craig, and this gin captures the enchanting magic of the sea. Unmistakably Hendrick's with an added infusion of locally sourced, coastal botanicals, Hendrick's Neptunia combines a sumptuously smooth, bright citrus finish with a delectably distinct yet distant sea breeze.

# FENNEL I APPLE

| | |
|---|---|
| CREATED BY | Liam Broom, Silverleaf, London |
| BAR | Stunning bar with elegant cocktails inspired by nature and the elements |
| DIFFICULTY LEVEL | Inordinately impressive (yet somehow still surprisingly simple) |
| MIXING METHOD | Stirred |
| STYLE | Up |
| GLASS | Nick & Nora |

## DESCRIPTION

*Inspired by the seaside, the botanicals in Hendrick's Neptunia are lifted by the salinity of the Fino sherry, the savoury anise notes of the fennel, the bright green notes from the apples and the base citrus notes from the orange bitters.*

## INGREDIENTS

- 1⅓ ounces (40 ml) Hendrick's Neptunia Gin
- ⅔ ounce (20 ml) Fino sherry
- 1 ounce (30 ml) fennel and apple cordial (see p. 231)
- 2 dashes of orange bitters

## DIRECTIONS

- Stir all the ingredients together with ice for 20 seconds.
- Strain into a chilled Nick & Nora glass or stemmed glass.

# HENDRICK'S WILDGARDEN CUP

| | |
|---:|:---|
| CREATED BY | Tim Pryde, Hendrick's Gin Palace Ambassador |
| DIFFICULTY LEVEL | Exceedingly easy |
| MIXING METHOD | Built and stirred |
| STYLE | Long |
| GLASS | Highball |

### DESCRIPTION

*Raspberries and Hendrick's Flora Adora are a wildly satisfying match. Hendrick's Wildgarden Cup is Hendrick's Flora Adora mixed long with a refreshing lemon soda and finished with a flourish of cooling cucumber, fresh mint and juicy raspberries.*

### INGREDIENTS

- **1¾ ounces (50 ml)** Hendrick's Flora Adora Gin
- **1 ounce (30 ml)** lemon juice
- **1 ounce (30 ml)** simple syrup (see p. 224)
- Soda
- **4** raspberries
- **5 or 6** mint leaves
- *3 thinly sliced rounds of cucumber and a mint sprig to garnish*

### DIRECTIONS

- Add all the ingredients to a highball glass.
- Stir gently to combine.
- Garnish with cucumber and a mint sprig.

### HENDRICK'S FLORA ADORA
#### RELEASED 2023

Hendrick's Flora Adora is a limited-release gin from Hendrick's Cabinet of Curiosities that's inspired by the enticing flowers that attract all manner of flying things to pollinate our precious ecosystem.

Our master distiller, Lesley Gracie, finds watching the butterflies and bees at work endlessly fascinating and has used the floral scents that they adore the most in Hendrick's Flora Adora. This delightful liquid is infused with an enticingly fresh floral bouquet and is the go-to gin for garden get-togethers, both big and small.

# HENDRICK'S CLOVER CLUB

DIFFICULTY LEVEL   Absurdly effortless
MIXING METHOD      Shaken
STYLE              Up
GLASS              Coupe

---

### DESCRIPTION

*There's a lot to love about the Clover Club cocktail. This rich, fruity little number is always a crowd pleaser. It looks elegantly appetising, has a wonderful velvety texture from the frothy egg white and the raspberry will ravish your taste buds. Raspberries in those summer months are spot-on – a little bit of sweetness with just the right amount of lip-smacking acidity.*

---

## INGREDIENTS

- 1¾ **ounces (50 ml)** Hendrick's Flora Adora Gin
- 1 **ounce (30 ml)** lemon juice, freshly squeezed
- ⅔ **ounce (20 ml)** raspberry syrup
- 1 egg white
- *3 raspberries to garnish*

## DIRECTIONS

- Combine all the ingredients in a cocktail shaker.
- Add ice and shake very well for 15–30 seconds.
- Strain into a chilled coupe.
- *Garnish with 3 raspberries on a skewer.*

## TOP TIP

The egg white doesn't add to the flavour but it really helps give that delicious velvety texture and attractive froth. To get a nice frothy head without overdiluting the drink, you could dry shake. Dry shaking means shaking the ingredients without ice for around 10–15 seconds before adding ice, then shaking for another 10–15 seconds. For those who don't want to use egg and the vegans among you, aquafaba will do a very similar job to egg white.

# Curious flavours from around the world

*The world is pretty much a kitchen cabinet, with different and unique flavours emerging from every little corner. As bartenders look to push the boundaries of cocktails, more and more of these ingredients are making their way into your local cocktail bar. This chapter puts some of these ingredients under the spotlight with recipes that'll take you on a journey of flavour from the floral notes of jasmine to the grassy, tropical feeling of pandan.*

DILL – THE DISTILLER'S BREW

LEMON VERBENA – PHILOSOPHER'S PUNCH

MAKRUT LIME LEAF – LYCHEE & LIME LEAF GIMLET

PANDAN – PANDAN

EUCALYPTUS – MARTOIL-Y

SUGAR SNAP PEAS – SEABIRD

JASMINE – FLORA

SHISO - FROM SINGAPORE TO YOKOHAMA

SENCHA – GIRVAN GIMLET

PINE – FOREST FIZZ

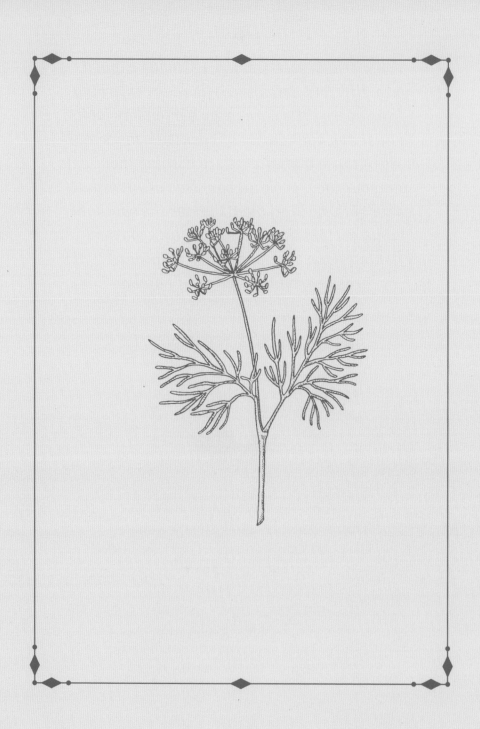

# DILL

*Dill is an ingredient I absolutely love. Native to both southeast Europe and southwest Asia, it pops up in recipes across the globe. The first flavour you might think of is pickle but there's a lot going on flavour-wise here, so don't let that guide you too much. Dill is part of the celery family and has some of the same characteristics – it's a little bit savoury, it's fresh and it's green – but it also has some unique anise quality in the background that can be really useful behind the bar.*

*cocktail recipe
overleaf*

# THE DISTILLER'S BREW

| | |
|---|---|
| CREATED BY | Mecanica, Manchester, England |
| BAR | A sumptuous classic cocktail bar serving extraordinary cocktails |
| DIFFICULTY LEVEL | Curiously complex |
| MIXING METHOD | Built |
| STYLE | Long |
| GLASS | Highball |

## DESCRIPTION

*This is a refreshing and refined highball. It's been inspired by Hendrick's master distiller Lesley Gracie, who used to brew teas from various plants and twigs as a child to serve to her family. The team at Mecanica have brought to life the quintessential British ritual of afternoon tea by combining the cucumber found in Hendrick's with an Earl Grey syrup and, of course, a dill shrub to replicate the notes from a cucumber and dill sandwich. That shrub twins wonderfully with the citrus notes found in Earl Grey tea in this easily replicable highball cocktail.*

## INGREDIENTS

- **1¾ ounces (50 ml)** Hendrick's Gin
- **1 ounce (30 ml)** Earl Grey syrup (see p. 224)
- **1 ounce (30 ml)** dill shrub (see p. 233)
- **3⅓ ounces (100 ml)** soda water
- *Sprig of dill to garnish*

## DIRECTIONS

- Add all the ingredients to a highball glass and fill with ice.
- Garnish with a sprig of dill.

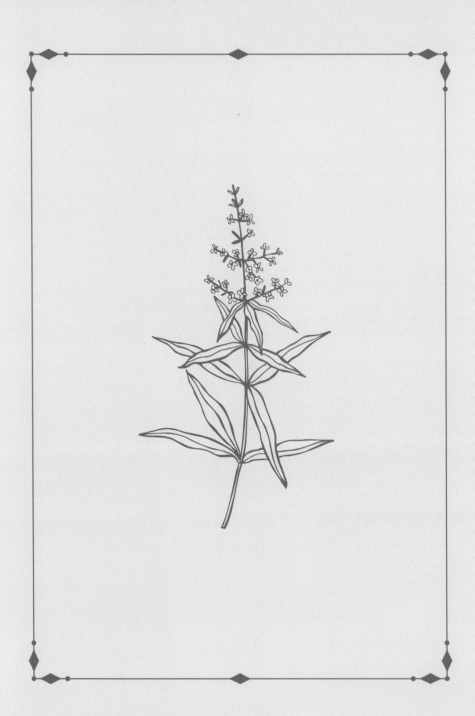

# LEMON VERBENA

*Lemon verbena was thought by many to have magical properties – the ability both to keep people away and to draw them close. The Romans used lemon verbena as offerings to the god of war to drive away the enemy, while others used it in love potions, or in cleansing spells to remove malevolent energy. But we're principally concerned with what flavours it adds. As the name suggests, it has an intense lemony character and yet it is also floral and fresh, adding so much vibrance to cocktails.*

*cocktail recipe
overleaf*

# PHILOSOPHER'S PUNCH

| | |
|---|---|
| CREATED BY | Simone De Luca, The Hoxton Hotel, Rome |
| BAR | A great spot for coffee, cocktails and bites around the clock – aperitivo hour is not to be missed |
| DIFFICULTY LEVEL | Inordinately impressive (yet somehow still surprisingly simple) |
| MIXING METHOD | Built |
| STYLE | Up |
| GLASS | Coupe |

### DESCRIPTION

*The Philosopher's Punch was inspired by the Greek philosophers Empedocles and Aristotle, who believed the elements were geometric forms. A cube was assigned to earth. In alchemy, earth was believed to be primarily 'dry', and secondarily 'cold'. Beyond those classical attributes, the chemical substance 'salt' was associated with earth. A couple of these tasty beverages will channel the inner philosopher that lies inside you.*

## INGREDIENTS

- **1¼ ounces (37.5 ml)** Hendrick's Gin
- **¾ ounce (22.5 ml)** Ouzo 12
- **½ ounce (15 ml)** Roots Rakomelo
- **1 ounce (30 ml)** salted kumquat sherbet (see p. 227)
- **1 ounce (30 ml)** lemon juice
- **1 ounce (30 ml)** lemon verbena tea (cooled)

## DIRECTIONS

- Combine all the ingredients in a mixing glass and serve in a coupe.

# MAKRUT LIME LEAF

*Makrut limes are usually found in Southeast Asia. The fruit itself has a really unique bumpy texture and on the stem is a glossy leaf that finds its way into all sorts of dishes and drinks, especially in Thai cuisine. We grow makrut limes in the Hendrick's Gin Palace hothouses and we're constantly using their leaves to create cocktails, as the flavour is really fantastic. They're rich, aromatic and fragrant, with almost a little bit of tanginess to them. Stick them in a curry or stick them in a cocktail. Better still, do both and enjoy them side by side.*

*cocktail recipe
overleaf*

# LYCHEE & LIME LEAF GIMLET

| | |
|---|---|
| CREATED BY | Barney Toy at Clipper, Auckland, New Zealand |
| BAR | This elegant bar celebrates the glamour of the golden era of international travel |
| DIFFICULTY LEVEL | Inordinately impressive (yet somehow still surprisingly simple) |
| MIXING METHOD | Shaken |
| STYLE | Up |
| GLASS | Nick & Nora or coupe |

## DESCRIPTION

*The Gimlet is one of my favourite gin cocktails – tangy and refreshing,*
*it allows the gin to shine through. This twist on a Gimlet by Barney Toy*
*at Clipper makes use of what would be leftover lime leaves from the bar's*
*garnish preparations to create a light, bright, floral cocktail.*
*The result is delicious.*

### INGREDIENTS

- 1¼ **ounces (37.5 ml)** Hendrick's Gin
- ⅔ **ounce (20 ml)** lychee syrup
- ⅓ **ounce (10 ml)** lime leaf cordial (see p. 230)
- ⅓ **ounce (10 ml)** lime juice
- 5 dashes of Boston bitters
- *Lime leaf coin to garnish*

### DIRECTIONS

- Combine all the ingredients in a shaker.
- Add ice and shake for 10–15 seconds.
- Fine-strain into a chilled Nick & Nora glass or a coupe.
- Garnish with a lime leaf coin.

# PANDAN

*Pandan is a plant with spiky green leaves that thrives in tropical climes. It is desired for its powerful and distinctive aromatics – think grassy vanilla meets rose and almond with a touch of coconut. You should be able to find it in a Southeast Asian food market or specialist food store. In that part of the world it's often used in desserts, partly for its flavour and partly for the distinctive green colour it can give to a dish.*

*cocktail recipe
overleaf*

# PANDAN

| | |
|---|---|
| CREATED BY | Yann Bouvignies, Scarfes Bar, London, England |
| BAR | A playful art-inspired bar with simple yet sophisticated drinks |
| DIFFICULTY LEVEL | Inordinately impressive (yet somehow still surprisingly simple) |
| MIXING METHOD | Stirred |
| STYLE | Up |
| GLASS | Nick & Nora or coupe |

## DESCRIPTION

*This is a crisp, clean, unique cocktail that shows off the pandan wonderfully. Those grassy, more floral notes of the pandan come to life with Hendrick's Gin.*

## INGREDIENTS

- **1¼ ounces (37.5 ml)** Hendrick's Gin
- **1 ounce (30 ml)** pandan cordial (see p. 230)
- **⅓ ounce (10 ml)** Fino sherry

## DIRECTIONS

- Place all the ingredients in a mixing glass with ice.
- Stir the ice for 20 seconds.
- Strain into a chilled Nick & Nora or coupe glass.

# EUCALYPTUS

*Loved by humans and koala bears alike, eucalyptus has a brilliant piney, citrus note with a little bit of minty freshness thrown in for good measure. The sinus-clearing refreshing scent that it is known for is great for drinks because it can add a really nice zing to proceedings. Native to Australia, where they dominate the landscape, there are somewhere in the region of 660 varieties of eucalyptus, and it's used for everything from medicinal purposes to cooking.*

*cocktail recipe
overleaf*

# MARTOIL-Y

| | |
|---|---|
| CREATED BY | Rory Shepherd at Little Red Door, Paris, France |
| BAR | A farm-to-glass cocktail bar playfully pushing boundaries |
| DIFFICULTY LEVEL | Inordinately impressive (yet somehow still surprisingly simple) |
| MIXING METHOD | Stirred |
| STYLE | Up |
| GLASS | Coupe or stemmed glass |

---

### DESCRIPTION

·

*This is a tantalising, tongue-tingling menthol Martini where the complexity of Hendrick's Orbium shines when combined with the cooling, cleansing sweetness of eucalyptus and peppermint, giving a green botanical backbone.*

---

## INGREDIENTS

- **1½ ounces (45 ml)** Hendrick's Orbium Gin
- **1½ tsps (7.5 ml)** eucalyptus and lemon thyme cordial (see p. 229)
- **½ ounce (15 ml)** Baldoria dry vermouth
- **½ ounce (15 ml)** Ricqlès peppermint oil
- *Drop of eucalyptus oil to garnish*

## DIRECTIONS

- Add all the ingredients into a mixing glass.
- Stir for 20 seconds.
- Strain into a chilled coupe or stemmed glass.
- Garnish with a drop of eucalyptus oil.

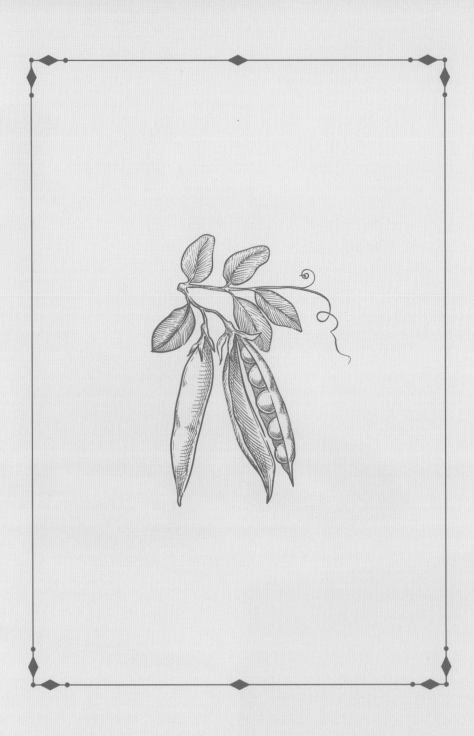

# SUGAR SNAP PEAS

*Sugar snap peas are a climbing plant, a cross between snow peas and your traditional garden pea. They're hidden inside a pod, which you can actually eat, and have a wonderfully green, fresh and sweet flavour to them. When you add them to drinks, that fresh sweetness really comes to life, especially in things like cordials. Peas themselves have been around since the Neolithic era but the sugar snap pea is a much more recent arrival, popping its head up in the 17th century.*

*cocktail recipe
overleaf*

# SEABIRD

| | |
|---|---|
| CREATED BY | Kyle Jamieson, Nauticus, Edinburgh, Scotland |
| BAR | A smashing cocktail bar situated in the heart of Leith, which is all about championing Scottish liquor and produce. So, naturally, they are a fan of Hendrick's Gin |
| DIFFICULTY LEVEL | Inordinately impressive (yet somehow still surprisingly simple) |
| MIXING METHOD | Shaken |
| STYLE | Up |
| GLASS | Wine |

### DESCRIPTION

*This herbal drink has a tang of fresh sweetness from the sugar snap peas and pineapple and a lovely effervesce from the sparkling wine.*

## INGREDIENTS

- **1¼ ounces (37.5 ml)** Hendrick's Gin
- **⅔ ounce (20 ml)** sugar snap pea and pineapple cordial (see p. 231)
- **⅓ ounce (10 ml)** Sweetdram Escubac
- **1 barspoon** Kummel
- **½ ounce (15 ml)** lemon juice
- Sparkling wine
- *3 thinly sliced rounds of cucumber to garnish*

## DIRECTIONS

- Shake all the ingredients (except the sparkling wine) in a cocktail shaker over ice.
- Strain into an ice-filled wine glass.
- Top with sparkling wine.
- Garnish with 3 thin slices of cucumber.

# JASMINE

*Jasmine flowers have a sweet, fruity and wonderful flavour. The plant was originally found in India but now grows in various parts of north and east Asia, as well as across Europe. It has beautiful white flowers and is revered for its intoxicating aromatics, so you'll find it cropping up in perfumes and having a devastatingly delicious effect in cocktails. You'll also commonly find it in jasmine tea, which is a blend of either white, black or green tea leaves and jasmine blossoms.*

*cocktail recipe*
*overleaf*

# FLORA

| | |
|---|---|
| CREATED BY | Hyacinthe Lescoët, The Cambridge Public House, Paris |
| BAR | Hidden away in the Marais, The Cambridge Public House was founded by three friends who lived and worked together in London. It's got the welcoming feel of a British pub combined with the service and ambience of a Parisian cocktail bar |
| DIFFICULTY LEVEL | Inordinately impressive (yet somehow still surprisingly simple) |
| MIXING METHOD | Stirred |
| STYLE | Up |
| GLASS | Coupe or small wine glass |

---

### DESCRIPTION

•

*This is a wonderfully floral and really elegant cocktail. Think of it as a White Negroni without the bitterness. The jasmine cordial pushes this cocktail into a deep floral place, which works fantastically well.*

---

INGREDIENTS

- **1 ounce (30 ml)** Hendrick's Orbium Gin
- **1 ounce (30 ml)** jasmine cordial (see p. 231)
- **1 ounce (30 ml)** dry vermouth (we recommend Dolin)
- *Jasmine sprig to garnish*

DIRECTIONS

- Place all the ingredients in a mixing glass.
- Stir over ice for 20 seconds.
- Fine-strain into a chilled coupe or small wine glass.
- Garnish with a jasmine sprig.

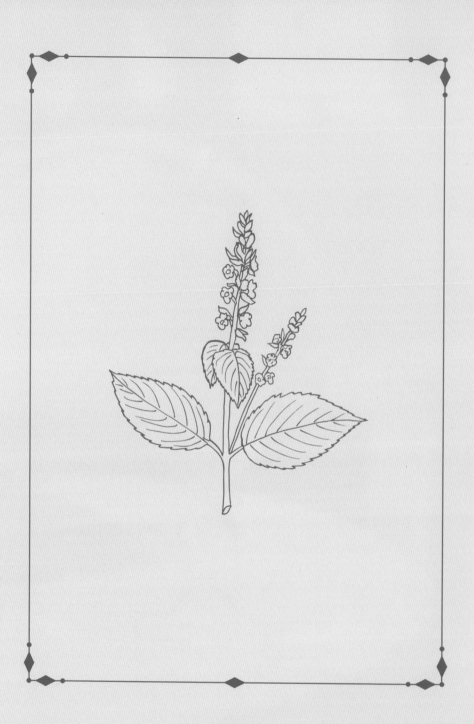

# SHISO

*Shiso is a Japanese herb that is part of the mint family. The leaves are ruffly on the outside and the herb can be found in both green and red varieties. The green variety is slightly more fresh in flavour while the red is slightly more bitter. You'll generally find them in Japanese cooking but they also taste amazing in cocktails, with their captivating bright flavour that has a little touch of earthiness to it. Depending on your location, these can be a little tricky to find fresh but you can find them somewhere online and they're absolutely worth the effort.*

*cocktail recipe
overleaf*

# FROM SINGAPORE TO YOKOHAMA

|  |  |
|---|---|
| CREATED BY | Rojanat Chareonsri, #FindTheLockerRoom, Bangkok, Thailand |
| BAR | #FindTheLockerRoom is a dream team project from some of the brightest minds on the Asian cocktail scene. You can find them making inventive cocktails, if you can navigate your way past a bank of steel lockers |
| DIFFICULTY LEVEL | Inordinately impressive (yet somehow still surprisingly simple) |
| MIXING METHOD | Shaken |
| STYLE | Up |
| GLASS | Coupe |

---

### DESCRIPTION

*From Singapore to Yokohama is a twist on a classic cocktail from Harry Craddock's famous Savoy Cocktail Book, called the Million Dollar Cocktail. It's a richly indulgent, tropical treat with a velvety smooth feel. The addition of shiso here adds a different dimension and depth to this classic cocktail, the origin of which is hotly debated. Some credit a Singapore bartender from the early 20th century, while others say it was invented by a bartender from the Grand Hotel in Yokohama, Japan – hence the name.*

---

## INGREDIENTS

- **1 ounce (30 ml)** Hendrick's Gin infused with shiso (see p. 232)
- **1 ounce (30 ml)** fresh pineapple juice
- **½ ounce (15 ml)** fresh lemon juice
- **½ ounce (15 ml)** Earl Grey syrup (see p. 224)
- **⅓ ounce (10 ml)** crème de cassis
- **½ ounce (15 ml)** egg whites
- *1 dash of Angostura aromatic bitters to garnish*

## DIRECTIONS

- Add all the ingredients to a shaker without any ice and dry shake to break up the egg whites.
- Then add ice and shake again.
- Double-strain into a coupe.
- Finish with a dash of Angostura bitters across the egg white foam.

# SENCHA

*Sencha green tea is the most popular drink in Japan. It has this amazing mix of sweetness, umami and astringency. Japanese sencha tends to have a refreshing character to it, and can often be green, vegetal, seaweedy or grassy. This makes it a great choice for the Girvan Gimlet, inspired by the lush green surroundings and coastline near our beloved Gin Palace on the rugged Ayrshire coast.*

*cocktail recipe
overleaf*

# GIRVAN GIMLET

| | |
|---|---|
| CREATED BY | Philipp Fröhlich, Trisoux Bar, Munich, Germany |
| BAR | A striking cocktail bar in the heart of Munich |
| DIFFICULTY LEVEL | Curiously complex |
| MIXING METHOD | Shaken |
| STYLE | On the rocks |
| GLASS | Rocks |

## DESCRIPTION

•

*Philipp Fröhlich was inspired to make this drink after visiting us at the Hendrick's Gin Palace in Girvan, Scotland, and being captivated by the lush green surroundings. The beautiful landscape, the salty sea breeze and the citrus trees in Lesley's greenhouse (alongside a host of other herbs and plants) encapsulate the feelings, smells and tastes during his magical two-day tour. This Girvan Gimlet is as cool as a cucumber – fresh, green and vibrant.*

### INGREDIENTS

- **1¾ ounces (50 ml)** Hendrick's Gin
- **1 ounce (30 ml)** sencha-herbs cordial (see p. 229)
- **⅓ ounce (10 ml)** fresh lemon juice
- **⅓ ounce (10 ml)** Fino sherry
- **2 dashes of saline solution** (see p. 223)
- *Cucumber curl to garnish*

### DIRECTIONS

- Combine all the ingredients in a shaker and fill with ice.
- Shake for 10–15 seconds.
- Strain and pour into a rocks glass.
- Add a cucumber curl to garnish.

# PINE

*The pine tree is an ingredient that you might overlook when it comes to cooking or making cocktails, but it's absolutely bursting with flavour, available all year round and perfect for using in gin cocktails. It has a lovely uplifting aroma and a distinctive refreshing quality, being a little bit herbal, a little bit perfumed and really complex. The Druids used to burn Scots pine during the Winter Solstice to celebrate the changing of the seasons, and whole forests of evergreen pine were decorated with shiny lights, not unlike a modern Christmas tree.*

*cocktail recipe
overleaf*

# FOREST FIZZ

| | |
|---|---|
| CREATED BY | Iain Townsend Griffiths |
| DIFFICULTY LEVEL | Curiously complex |
| MIXING METHOD | Built |
| STYLE | Long |
| GLASS | Highball |

## DESCRIPTION

•

*This drink is the perfect festive concoction, ideal for sipping before
a celebratory dinner with friends. The pine finds its way into the drink
within a Champagne and pine needle syrup – all those wonderful oils that
you find inside the pine needles go wonderfully with the dry, crisp notes
from the wine. This syrup is combined with some pommeau, an aperitif from
Normandy that combines apple juice and apple brandy, which really brings
out some of the more fruity notes in the Champagne and pine syrup.*

### INGREDIENTS

- **4½ ounces (135 ml)** Hendrick's Gin
- **2¼ ounces (65 ml)** citric acid
  solution (see p. 223)
- **2¼ ounces (65 ml)** Champagne and
  pine needle syrup (see p. 225)
- **1¾ ounces (50 ml)** pommeau
- **½ ounce (15 ml)** ginger eau de vie
- **1¼ ounces (37.5 ml)** filtered water
- **4½ ounces (135 ml)** soda water
- *Orange twist to garnish*

### DIRECTIONS

- Grab yourself a clean, empty 3-cup
  (750 ml) glass bottle.
- Use a funnel to add all the
  ingredients (except the soda water.)
- Leave in your fridge to chill for at
  least 3 hours.
- To serve, pour into a chilled rocks
  glass filled with ice and top up with
  soda water.
- Garnish with an orange twist.

### TOP TIP

Champagne syrup is the perfect way
to use any leftover fizz you might
have, even after it's gone flat. You can
also make syrups with leftover wine.

# Curiously complex

*This is a collection of trickier cocktails featuring harder-to-come-by ingredients and fancier equipment. It is a chapter for people who are already good at making cocktails at home and want to challenge themselves a bit.*

EL BIERZO

BALSAMICO

MIDNIGHT BREKKIE

PINAL

CAPRESE

GOLDEN CHARM

ROSALINE

EARL OF GIRVAN

# EL BIERZO

CREATED BY    Mario Villalón, Angelita Madrid, Spain
DIFFICULTY LEVEL    Curiously complex
MIXING METHOD    Stirred
STYLE    Up
GLASS    Coupe

### DESCRIPTION

*This is an elegant, tangy tribute to one of Spain's most glorious wines, the Godello. The Godello is a lesser-known grape that nearly disappeared into oblivion but has since been revived. Mario from Angelita Madrid, which serves an excellent array of Spanish wines, crazy good cocktails and the best tomatoes known to man, has developed this complex, creative cocktail that complements the green, refreshing notes of Hendrick's Gin and makes the wine the star of the show. This cocktail calls for some curious ingredients, such as citric acid solution (a professional bartender alternative to fresh lemon and lime) and mastic liqueur, a Greek liquor with cedar and pine notes. This is definitely one for the more adventurous among you.*

## INGREDIENTS

- **2 ounces (60 ml)** Godello white wine
- **½ ounce (15 ml)** Hendrick's Gin
- **⅓ ounce (10 ml)** mastic liqueur
- **⅓ ounce (10 ml)** celery syrup (see p. 224)
- **½ ounce (15 ml)** citric acid solution (see p. 223)
- **1 ml** saline solution (see p. 223)
- **5** parsley leaves
- **5** mint leaves

## DIRECTIONS

- Combine all the ingredients in a mixing glass and add ice.
- Stir gently for 20 seconds.
- Strain into a chilled coupe.

### TOP TIP

You'll want to keep the drink as cold as possible, so chill your glass to prevent it warming up the drink.

# BALSAMICO

| | |
|---|---|
| CREATED BY | Elliot Ball, Cocktail Trading Co., London, England |
| BAR | A bar founded by a trio of lifelong bartenders dedicated to developing really tasty drinks |
| DIFFICULTY LEVEL | Curiously complex |
| MIXING METHOD | Stirred |
| STYLE | Up |
| GLASS | Martini or coupe |

## DESCRIPTION

*This is a delicious savoury twist on a Martini which plays with the idea of a vinaigrette. Like salad leaves, Martinis have a habit of being distinctly under-seasoned, especially when made at home, and vinaigrettes such as soy, vinegar and elderflower have a natural affinity with the cucumber in Hendrick's.*

## INGREDIENTS

- 1¾ **ounces (50 ml)** Hendrick's Gin
- ¾ **ounce (22.5 ml)** elderflower cordial
- **1 ml** light soy sauce
- **1 ml** white balsamic
- ½ **ounce (15 ml)** walnut liqueur (such as Noix de la Saint Jean)
- ⅓–½ **ounce (10–15 ml)** dessert wine, depending on sweetness
- *Spritz of lemon oil to garnish*

## DIRECTIONS

- Combine all the ingredients and stir over ice until perfectly cold.
- Strain and pour into a Martini glass or coupe.
- Garnish with a spritz of lemon oil.

## TOP TIP

A steady hand is required here, as being delicate with the soy and balsamic is the difference between a curiously delicious twist and a drink that is interesting for all the wrong reasons.

When stirring over ice, take the ice out of the freezer for a little while first, as ice fresh from the freezer will have frost on it that will add to the dilution. Ideally, you want the ice to be frost-free and clear, and if it sits out on the counter for 10–20 minutes it will be.

Chill your Martini glass or coupe in the freezer or with a cube of ice before pouring to avoid the temperature of the glass warming your perfectly chilled drink.

# MIDNIGHT BREKKIE

| | |
|---|---|
| CREATED BY | Pankaj Balachandran, Tesouro, Goa, India |
| BAR | Super-vibey, relaxed bar smashing out seriously good drinks |
| DIFFICULTY LEVEL | Curiously complex |
| MIXING METHOD | Blended |
| STYLE | On the rocks |
| GLASS | Rocks |

## DESCRIPTION

*This cocktail came about during lockdown, when Pankaj was working on various remote projects late at night while munching on peanut butter and jelly sandwiches. This midnight snack became the inspiration for a drink, with a little international help via the magic of Zoom, as Pankaj figured out how to make peanut butter and jelly in liquid form. This curious combination proved so popular that Pankaj was soon batching and bottling it. Eight months later, at his bar in Goa, it became their best-selling drink by far and is now a regular fixture on the menu.*

## INGREDIENTS

### SERVES 6–8

- 4 ounces (120 ml) strawberry syrup
- 1¾ tbs (25 g) peanut butter
- 6¾ ounces (200 ml) watermelon juice
- 2 cups (500 ml) Hendrick's Gin
- 3⅓ ounces (100 ml) Martini Bianco
- 6 ounces (175 ml) malic acid
- *Watermelon slices to garnish*

## DIRECTIONS

- Put the strawberry syrup, peanut butter and watermelon juice in a blender and blitz until all the peanut butter is mixed well with the liquid.
- Mix the Hendrick's Gin, Martini Bianco and malic acid together with the peanut butter and jelly mixture.
- Rest the mixture in the fridge for half an hour.
- Strain the mixture through

# PINAL

CREATED BY | Alexander Ramirez, Café Dragón, Medellín, Colombia
BAR | A beautiful bar where the flavours of childhood are experimented with and turned into new and exciting ingredients – from fermented fruit cordials to herbal tinctures
DIFFICULTY LEVEL | Curiously complex
MIXING METHOD | Stirred
STYLE | On the rocks
GLASS | Rocks

## DESCRIPTION

*The inspiration for Alexander Ramirez's drink was the magical aroma of the forest, which instantly transports him back to fun times growing up. Scent is so powerful and has an incredible way of evoking memories and sensations, allowing you to travel through time and space. Fresh, clean and cold, this cocktail encapsulates that sensation of being in the forest with the green aroma all around, the coldness of the trees, the clear sky, the pungent pine – that is pinal!*

## INGREDIENTS

- 1½ ounces (45 ml) Hendrick's Gin
- ¾ ounce (22.5 ml) herbal cordial (see p. 228)
- 2 ounces (60 ml) Pinot Grigio
- *Pine needles to garnish*

## DIRECTIONS

- Stir the Hendrick's Gin, herbal cordial and Pinot Grigio over ice for 30 seconds.
- Drill a hole into a fresh ice cube with some sharp implement.
- Insert the pine needles inside the hole and place inside a rocks glass.
- Strain the cocktail over the ice.

## TOP TIP

What makes this curiously complex is the show-stopping garnish. It's not actually that difficult to create, but it does take a little effort, which pays off with the compliments this drink will receive.

# CAPRESE

CREATED BY
Eric van Beek, Handshake Speakeasy, Mexico City, Mexico

BAR
An incredibly creative bar hiding in plain sight. It's a small place but it's packed to the rafters every night and serves some of the best cocktails you could ever hope to find

DIFFICULTY LEVEL
Curiously complex

MIXING METHOD
Stirred

STYLE
Up

GLASS
Nick & Nora or stemmed glass

---

### DESCRIPTION

*One of the best Hendrick's cocktails I've ever tasted. It brings to life the flavours you'll find in a Caprese salad in a truly inventive way.*

---

### INGREDIENTS

- **2 ounces (60 ml)** Hendrick's Gin infused with basil (see p. 232)
- **1 ounce (30 ml)** tomato water cordial (see p. 229)

### DIRECTIONS

- Pour the ingredients into a mixing glass over ice.
- Stir and strain into a Nick & Nora or stemmed glass.

# GOLDEN CHARM

| | |
|---|---|
| CREATED BY | Shelley Tai, Nutmeg & Clove, Singapore |
| BAR | A renowned bar that pays homage to Singapore's rich cultural heritage and diversity and makes sure you'll learn a thing or two with every drink |
| DIFFICULTY LEVEL | Curiously complex |
| MIXING METHOD | Shaken |
| STYLE | Long |
| GLASS | Highball |

## DESCRIPTION

*A fruity and fresh concoction that accentuates the floral notes of Hendrick's Gin.*

### INGREDIENTS

- **1 ounce (30 ml)** Hendrick's Gin
- **⅔ ounce (20 ml)** pomelo shrub (see p. 233)
- **⅔ ounce (20 ml)** chamomile syrup (see p. 225)
- **½ ounce (15 ml)** lemon juice
- Ginger beer
- *Allspice berries and chamomile to garnish*

### DIRECTIONS

- Mix all the ingredients (except the ginger beer) in a shaker.
- Add ice and shake well for 10–15 seconds.
- Strain into a highball glass filled with ice.
- Top up with ginger beer.
- Garnish with allspice berries and chamomile.

# ROSALINE

| | |
|---|---|
| CREATED BY | Paolo Maffietti, Maybe Sammy, Sydney, Australia |
| BAR | A beautiful, fun cocktail bar serving elegant drinks |
| DIFFICULTY LEVEL | Curiously complex |
| MIXING METHOD | Built |
| STYLE | Long |
| GLASS | Highball |

## DESCRIPTION

*Rosaline is a character in* Romeo and Juliet *who is the romantic interest of Romeo before he meets Juliet. The name Rosaline is thought to be from the Latin* Rosa linda, *which roughly translates as 'lovely rose'. This drink takes inspiration from Rosaline's character, the perfect subject for a cocktail that highlights the floral notes of the rose found in Hendrick's Gin and has a smoky aftertaste, representing how she disappears as the tragedy unfolds.*

## INGREDIENTS

- **1 ounce (30 ml)** Hendrick's Gin
- **½ ounce (15 ml)** Fino sherry (we recommend Tio Pepe)
- **⅔ ounce (20 ml)** smoked rose cordial (see p. 230)
- Fever Tree Mediterranean Tonic
- *Rose petals to garnish*

## DIRECTIONS

- Add all the ingredients to a highball glass.
- Add ice at the end.
- Garnish with rose petals.

# EARL OF GIRVAN

CREATED BY Kyle Jamieson, Nauticus, Edinburgh
BAR A smashing cocktail bar situated in the heart of Leith, which is all about championing Scottish liquor and produce. You did know that Hendrick's Gin is Scottish, right?
DIFFICULTY LEVEL Curiously complex
MIXING METHOD Built
STYLE On the rocks
GLASS Rocks

## DESCRIPTION

*This is a single-serve punch-style drink where the lengthener is Earl Grey and pear cordial. There are layers of flavour going on here, with the richness from the Oloroso, and the bitterness of the tea is balanced by the sweetness of the pear and fruity citrus.*

### INGREDIENTS

- 1⅓ ounces (40 ml) Hendrick's Gin
- ½ ounce (15 ml) Oloroso sherry
- ½ ounce (15 ml) Earl Grey and pear cordial (see p. 228)
- ½ tsp (2.5 ml) citric acid solution (see p. 223)
- *Spritz of orange blossom water to garnish*

### DIRECTIONS

- Add all the ingredients to a shaker and shake with ice.
- Strain into a rocks glass with ice.
- Spritz with orange blossom water.

# PART 3

·

# DIY

# Important ingredients

MAKING YOUR OWN sugar syrups, cordials, sodas and infusions can be an incredibly fun way to get creative with your cocktails, and it's also much easier than you'd think. Many of the recipes in this book have been rustled up by some of the best bartenders in the world, and some include bespoke cordials, syrups, shrubs, infusions and even a vinegar and an oleo saccharum. Think of these as the cocktail alternative of stocks, or sauces and seasonings in the food world, as they allow you to take your creations into exciting new areas of flavour.

To get to grips with it all, you'll need to know how to make a simple syrup. Once you understand this then the other recipes are simply adaptations of that base recipe. After you've made your syrups or cordials, let them cool down before putting them in a clean sealed container or sterilised glass bottle and into the fridge. Syrups or cordials will tend to keep for about two to three weeks if sealed, so you can get plenty of use out of them.

## CURIOUS FACT

*A shrub is not just a plant or bush. In cocktail terms, a shrub is a drinking vinegar, a non-alcoholic syrup that combines vinegar with sugar, fruit and flavourings to add a zesty zing to cocktails.*

You'll come across a few acids in some of these important ingredient recipes. Don't worry! These are incredibly versatile ingredients that allow bartenders to add precise amounts of acidity to recipes. Lemons, limes and oranges are fantastic, but they don't allow you a precise degree of control over the acidity. This is why many bartenders are switching to using citric and malic acid rather than fresh citrus fruits. These isolated acids allow bartenders to create a consistent product night after night – so every time you order the drink, no matter what the season, it tastes exactly the same. So if you're feeling adventurous, experiment with some of these acids in your homemade ingredients.

# SOLUTIONS

# WATERS

## SALINE SOLUTION

*A simple saltwater solution that can help to brighten up elements of sweet or sour drinks.*

### USED IN

El Bierzo (see p. 202)
Girvan Gimlet (see p. 194)

### INGREDIENTS

- **3⅓ ounces (100 ml)** water
- **¾ ounce (20 g)** fleur de Sel

### INSTRUCTIONS

- Heat the water and leave to cool until it is lukewarm.
- Dissolve the salt in the lukewarm water.
- Leave to cool, then pour into a clean glass bottle and keep in the fridge.

## CITRIC ACID SOLUTION

### USED IN

Forest Fizz (see p. 198),
El Bierzo (see p. 202) *and*
Earl of Girvan (see p. 216)

### INGREDIENTS

- **4 g** citric acid
- **3 g** malic acid
- **3 ounces (93 ml)** water

### INSTRUCTIONS

- Stir to combine the ingredients and store in a clean container.

## CUCUMBER WATER

### USED IN

Green Gimlet (see p. 119)

### INGREDIENTS

- **1** large cucumber
- **1¼ cups (300 ml)** water

### INSTRUCTIONS

- Peel the cucumber, cut lengthways into quarters and remove the seeds.
- Blend the cucumber until smooth and liquid.
- Combine the cucumber juice and water in a 1:3 ratio and, presto, you have cucumber water.

# SYRUPS

## SIMPLE SYRUP, AKA SUGAR SYRUP

INGREDIENTS

- **2 cups (500 ml) water**
- **2¼ pounds (1 kg) caster sugar**

INSTRUCTIONS

- Bring your water to a boil in a saucepan and then remove from the heat.
- Add your sugar and stir until it's dissolved. Leave to cool, then bottle. Simple!

## EARL GREY SYRUP

USED IN

The Distiller's Brew (see p. 162) *and* From Singapore to Yokohama (see p. 190)

INGREDIENTS

- **3½ ounces (100 ml) boiling water**
- **¼ ounce (8 g) Earl Grey tea**
- **¾ ounce (20 g) caster sugar**

INSTRUCTIONS

- Add the boiling water to the tea in a heatproof jug.
- Allow the tea to steep in the water for 10 minutes.
- Strain into a clean jug and allow the liquid to cool.
- Add the caster sugar and stir until dissolved.
- Leave to cool, then bottle.

## CELERY SYRUP

USED IN

July Hula (see p. 82)
El Bierzo (see p. 202)

INGREDIENTS

- **7 ounces (200 g) celery**
- **2½ cups (600 ml) water**
- **2¼ pounds (1 kg) sugar**

INSTRUCTIONS

- Chop the celery into chunks, combine with the water in a blender and blend until smooth.
- Add all the ingredients to a saucepan and gently heat until all the sugar is dissolved.
- Leave to cool, then strain and bottle.

## BEETROOT SYRUP

USED IN

Neptune's Secret (see p. 150)

INGREDIENTS

- **8½ ounces (250 ml) beetroot juice**
- **7 ounces (200 g) granulated sugar**

INSTRUCTIONS

- Combine the ingredients in a saucepan and bring to a boil.
- When the sugar is dissolved, remove from the heat and allow to cool.
- Strain with a fine strainer, then bottle.

## CHAMOMILE SYRUP

USED IN

Golden Charm (see p. 213)

INGREDIENTS

- 2 cups (500 ml) just-boiled water
- ¾ ounce (20 g) chamomile flowers
- 17⅔ ounces (500 g) sugar

INSTRUCTIONS

- Pour boiling water into a heatproof bowl, add the chamomile flowers and allow them to steep in the water for 10 minutes.
- Strain, then add the sugar.
- Stir to dissolve.
- Leave to cool, then bottle.

## TARRAGON SYRUP

USED IN

Solstice Swing (see p. 143)

INGREDIENTS

- 1¼ cups (300 ml) just-boiled water
- 1 ounce (30 g) tarragon
- 10½ ounces (300 g) sugar

INSTRUCTIONS

- Pour the water into a heatproof bowl, add the tarragon and allow it to steep for 15 minutes.
- Remove the tarragon and add the sugar.
- Stir until dissolved.
- Leave to cool, then bottle.

## CHAMPAGNE AND PINE NEEDLE SYRUP

USED IN

Forest Fizz (see p. 198)

INGREDIENTS

- 6¾ ounces (200 ml) Champagne
- 7 ounces (200 g) caster sugar
- ¾ ounce (20 g) pine needles (removed from stem)

INSTRUCTIONS

- Combine the Champagne and caster sugar in a saucepan and place over a low heat.
- Stir slowly until the sugar is dissolved.
- Remove and leave to cool.
- Once cool, add the pine needles to the syrup and infuse for 2 hours.
- Strain and store in the fridge.

TOP TIP

Ideally, you'll want to grab your pine needles from Spruce or Douglas Fir trees. Their flavour is most intense during the spring but pick them as and when you need them. When using pine in drinks, you must take proper precautions to ensure the tree you're foraging from isn't being treated with any chemicals and you've properly identified it as a pine tree.

# BITTERS

# OLEO

## ATLANTIC BITTERS

USED IN

Atlantic Daisy (see p. 106)

INGREDIENTS

- **¾ ounce (20 g)** dried olive leaf
- **⅔ ounce (20 ml)** sesame oil
- **5 ounces (145 ml)** Regan's orange bitters

INSTRUCTIONS

- Mix all the ingredients together, cover and leave at room temperature for 4 hours.
- Store in the freezer overnight or until the oil solidifies.
- Strain through a coffee filter into a clean bottle.

## SALTED LEMON OLEO

USED IN

Green Gimlet (see p. 119)

INGREDIENTS

- Peel of **2** lemons
- **10½ ounces (300 g)** white granulated sugar
- **½ tsp** salt
- **1¼ cups (300 ml)** lemon juice

INSTRUCTIONS

- Use a vegetable peeler to remove the peel from the lemons and add it to the sugar and salt in a bowl.
- Use a muddler or a wooden spoon to crush the sugar, salt and peel together.
- Cover tightly and leave overnight in the fridge.
- Add the lemon juice and stir to dissolve.
- Strain through a coffee filter and store in the fridge.

# VINEGARS

## STRAWBERRY AND COCONUT VINEGAR

USED IN

Strawberry Gibson (see p. 56)

INGREDIENTS

- **7 ounces (200 g)** fresh strawberries
- **3½ ounces (100 g)** caster sugar
- **1¾ ounces (50 ml)** coconut vinegar
- 1 pinch of rock salt

INSTRUCTIONS

- Remove the strawberry stalks, chop and then combine with all the ingredients in a pan.
- Stir over a medium heat for about 5 minutes until the sugar is dissolved.
- Remove from the heat and leave to cool.
- Once cooled, strain through a coffee filter into a clean bottle.

## SALTED KUMQUAT SHERBET

USED IN

Philosopher's Punch (see p. 166)

INGREDIENTS

- **8¾ ounces (250 g)** kumquats
- **2¼ pounds (1 kg)** caster sugar
- **2.5 g** salt
- **2 cups (500 ml)** clementine juice

INSTRUCTIONS

- Wash the kumquats thoroughly and slice them in half.
- Combine the kumquats with the sugar and salt in a container and muddle them until all the pulp and the juice are coming out.
- Mix well and leave to rest in the fridge overnight.
- The next day, add the clementine juice, mix well, then pour the mixture into a pan and dissolve over a low heat.
- Strain when hot and then let the mixture cool and transfer to a clean bottle.

# CORDIALS

## HERBAL CORDIAL

USED IN

Pinal (see p. 209)

INGREDIENTS

- **½ cup (4 g)** dill
- **⅓ ounce (9 g)** lemon verbena
- **5 g** rue (a bitter leaf like sorrel or rocket will work if you can't find rue)
- **5⅓ ounces (150 g)** sugar
- **1 ounce (30 g)** lime peel
- **2 ounces (60 ml)** lime juice
- **2 ounces (60 ml)** warm water

INSTRUCTIONS

- Add all the herbs to a bowl with the sugar and gently muddle together.
- Add the lime peel and continue to muddle, releasing the aromatics.
- Cover the bowl and set aside for 8 hours.
- Add the lime juice and the warm water and stir to dissolve.
- Strain through a fine strainer into a clean bottle.

## EARL GREY AND PEAR CORDIAL

USED IN

Earl of Girvan (see p. 216)

INGREDIENTS

- **1 × 14-ounce (400 g)** tin of pears
- **6¾ ounces (200 ml)** water
- **3** Earl Grey tea bags
- **8¾ ounces (250 g)** caster sugar

INSTRUCTIONS

- Add the pears to a small saucepan.
- Simmer over a low heat, softly pressing the pears to extract flavour, until they're soft.
- Remove from the heat. Add the tea bags and infuse for 5 minutes.
- Fine-strain into a clean jug and add the caster sugar, stirring to dissolve.
- Transfer to a clean bottle.

## CUCUMBER AND WHITE WINE CORDIAL

USED IN

Artemisium Orbium (see p. 110)

INGREDIENTS

- 1¼ ounces (35 g) lime zest
- 2¼ pounds (1 kg) sugar
- 17⅔ ounces (500 g) cucumber (peeled and sliced)
- 2 cups (500 ml) dry, light white wine
- ⅓ ounce (10 g) citric acid powder

INSTRUCTIONS

- Add the lime zest to the sugar and leave to sit for 1 hour.
- Blend the cucumber and white wine in a blender.
- Combine both mixtures and stir to dissolve.
- Strain through a coffee filter into a clean jug.
- Add the citric acid and stir to dissolve.
- Transfer to a clean bottle.

## SENCHA-HERBS CORDIAL

USED IN

Girvan Gimlet (see p. 194)

INGREDIENTS

- 10 ounces (300 ml) sencha tea
- 6¾ ounces (200 ml) fresh lemon juice
- ½ pound (250 g) sugar
- ⅓ ounce (10 g) sage
- Peel of 1 lemon
- Peel of 2 cucumbers

INSTRUCTIONS

- Add the sencha tea, lemon juice and sugar to a saucepan and bring to a boil.
- Remove from heat and then add the sage, lemon peel and cucumber peel.
- Leave to cool, then strain using a fine strainer into a clean bottle.

## TOMATO WATER CORDIAL

USED IN

Caprese (see p. 210)

INGREDIENTS

- 2⅔ pounds (1.2 kg) cherry tomatoes
- ½ pound (250 g) caster sugar
- ½ ounce (14 g) citric acid powder
- 2.75 g tartaric acid powder

INSTRUCTIONS

- Blend the cherry tomatoes in a blender to a smooth pulp.
- Let the tomato pulp sit for 10 minutes, then run it through a coffee filter until you have clear tomato water. You should have around 2½ cups (600 ml).
- Mix the tomato water with the caster sugar, citric acid and tartaric acid.
- Strain and transfer to a clean bottle.

## EUCALYPTUS AND LEMON THYME CORDIAL

USED IN

Martoil-y (see p. 178)

INGREDIENTS

- ½ ounce (15 g) eucalyptus leaves
- 5 g lemon thyme
- 1¼ cups (300 ml) water
- ½ pound (250 g) caster sugar
- 1 g malic acid

INSTRUCTIONS

- Infuse the herbs with the water overnight.
- Strain through a coffee filter into a clean bowl, then add the sugar and acid.
- Stir to combine, then transfer to a clean bottle.

## PANDAN CORDIAL

USED IN

Pandan (see p. 174)

INGREDIENTS

- **2 cups (500 ml)** just-boiled water
- **⅓ ounce (10 g)** chamomile flowers
- **3¼ ounces (90 g)** fresh pandan leaves
- **17⅔ ounces (500 g)** caster sugar
- **½ ounce (13.5 g)** malic acid
- **¼ ounce (6.5 g)** citric acid

INSTRUCTIONS

- Pour boiling water into a bowl, add the chamomile flowers and brew for 15 minutes, then fine-strain.
- Chop the pandan leaves into 3–4cm pieces and infuse for 45 minutes in the chamomile water.
- Strain through a coffee filter into a jug, add the rest of the ingredients and stir to dissolve.
- Transfer to a clean bottle.

## LIME LEAF CORDIAL

USED IN

Lychee & Lime Leaf Gimlet (see p. 170)

INGREDIENTS

- **3½ ounces (100 g)** caster sugar
- **6¾ ounces (200 ml)** water
- **⅓ ounce (10 g)** lime leaf
- **2.5 g** malic acid
- **2.5 g** citric acid

INSTRUCTIONS

- Add the caster sugar, water and lime leaf to a saucepan and gently heat, stirring, for 10 minutes until the sugar is dissolved and lime leaf has infused the water.
- Leave to cool, then add the malic acid and citric acid.
- Stir to dissolve, then transfer to a clean bottle.

## PINEAPPLE CORDIAL

USED IN

Green Belt (see p. 62)

INGREDIENTS

- **3½ ounces (100 g)** caster sugar
- **2 cups (500 ml)** pineapple juice
- **5 g** citric acid
- **2.5 g** malic acid

INSTRUCTIONS

- Add the caster sugar and pineapple juice to a saucepan and gently heat, stirring until the sugar is dissolved.
- Leave to cool, then add the citric and malic acid, stir to dissolve and transfer to a clean bottle.

## SMOKED ROSE CORDIAL

USED IN

Rosaline (see p. 214)

INGREDIENTS

- **½ ounce (15 g)** Lapsang Souchong tea
- **2 cups (500 ml)** hot water
- **17⅔ ounces (500 g)** caster sugar
- **3 drops** rose essential oil
- **2.5 g** malic acid

INSTRUCTIONS

- Allow the Lapsang Souchong to infuse with the hot water for 12 minutes.
- Strain with a coffee filter into a jug.
- Add the sugar and stir to dissolve
- Then add the rose essential oil and malic acid and stir to dissolve.
- Transfer to a clean bottle.

## JASMINE CORDIAL

USED IN
Flora (see p. 186)

INGREDIENTS

- 2¾ cups (670 ml) water
- 1 ounce (30 g) fresh jasmine
- 7 ounces (200 g) caster sugar
- ⅓ ounce (9 g) citric acid

INSTRUCTIONS

- Boil the water, then pour it into a heatproof bowl and allow to cool for 5 minutes.
- Add the jasmine and steep for 10 minutes.
- Strain the water and discard the jasmine.
- Gently heat the water again in a saucepan, add the sugar and citric acid and stir until dissolved.
- Transfer to a clean bottle.

## FENNEL AND APPLE CORDIAL

USED IN
Fennel I Apple (see p. 153)

INGREDIENTS

- 4 Granny Smith apples
- 2 fennel bulbs

Per litre of juice add
- 1⅓ pounds (600 g) caster sugar
- ¼ ounce (8 g) citric acid
- ¼ ounce (8 g) malic acid

INSTRUCTIONS

- Peel and chop the apples and fennel bulbs and add to a juicer. You should have around 3 cups (750 ml) of liquid.
- Gently heat the juice in a saucepan, then add the caster sugar, citric acid and malic acid and stir until dissolved.
- Transfer to a clean bottle.

## SUGAR SNAP PEA AND PINEAPPLE CORDIAL

USED IN
Seabird (see p. 182)

INGREDIENTS

- 6¼ ounces (175 g) sugar snap peas
- 6¼ ounces (175 g) fresh pineapple
- 8½ ounces (250 ml) water
- 1⅓ pounds (600 g) caster sugar
- Pinch of salt

INSTRUCTIONS

- Blend all the ingredients except the sugar and salt.
- Strain through a coffee filter into a clean jug.
- Add the sugar and stir to combine.
- Add a pinch of salt.
- Transfer to a clean bottle.

# INFUSIONS

## HENDRICK'S GIN INFUSED WITH SHISO

USED IN

From Singapore to Yokohama
(see p. 190)

INGREDIENTS

- **10** shiso leaves
- **3 cups (700 ml)** Hendrick's Gin

INSTRUCTIONS

- Add the shiso leaves to a bottle of Hendrick's Gin.
- Freeze for 24 hours, then strain into a clean bottle.

## HENDRICK'S GIN INFUSED WITH BASIL

USED IN

Caprese (see p. 210)

INGREDIENTS

- **4½ cups (1 L)** Hendrick's Gin
- **2¾ ounces (80 g)** fresh Italian basil

INSTRUCTIONS

- Add the ingredients to a freezer bag, seal and freeze for 48 hours.
- Remove from the freezer and strain through a coffee filter into a clean bottle.

## GREEN CHILLI VODKA

USED IN

Green Belt (see p. 62)

INGREDIENTS

- **1** green chilli
- **3 cups (750 ml)** vodka (we love Reyka vodka)

INSTRUCTIONS

- Finely chop the green chilli and add it to a bottle of vodka.
- Put the bottle in the freezer for 24 hours.
- Strain the vodka using a fine strainer into a clean bottle.

# SHRUBS

## DILL SHRUB

USED IN
The Distiller's Brew (see p. 162)

The Distiller's Brew (see p. 162)

INGREDIENTS

- ⅔ ounce (18 g) fresh dill
- ⅔ ounce (20 ml) white wine vinegar
- 3⅓ ounces (100 ml) water
- 3½ ounces (100 g) caster sugar

INSTRUCTIONS

- Place all the ingredients in a jar and seal.
- Leave for 24 hours, then strain through a sieve to remove excess dill.
- Transfer to a clean bottle.

## POMELO SHRUB

USED IN
Golden Charm (see p. 213)

Golden Charm (see p. 213)

INGREDIENTS

- 2½ cups (600 ml) pomelo juice
- 2 ounces (60 g) allspice
- ¾ ounce (20 g) pomelo skin
- 15¼ ounces (450 ml) white vinegar
- 5 ounces (150 ml) water
- 1⅓ pounds (600 g) sugar

INSTRUCTIONS

- Combine all the ingredients in a glass jar.
- Mix well and let it sit for 3–5 days.
- Strain using a fine strainer or sieve.
- Transfer to a clean bottle.

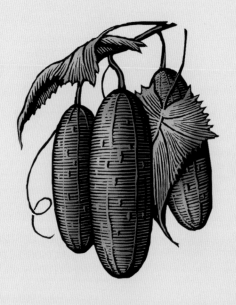

# Glorious cucumber garnishes

WE ABSOLUTELY DRINK with our eyes, and if a cocktail looks delicious then there's a good chance it'll taste great too. Garnishes won't only make your cocktails look incredible, they can also elevate the senses, enhance the experience and leave your guests' mouths watering before they have even taken their first glorious sip.

At Hendrick's Gin, we've always been known for our cucumber garnish. The garnish brings our gin to life wonderfully and is incredibly simple to make. There's much more to the cucumber than a slice, so here are some garnish tips that will help you take things to the next level.

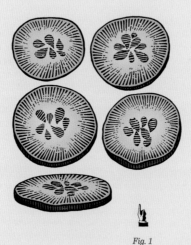

*Fig. 1*

*Fig. 2*

### THE SIGNATURE SLICE *(Fig. 1)*

A thin, round slice of cucumber that'll fit perfectly in your Gin & Tonic as well as many of the cocktails you'll find in this book. Simply slice a thin round of cucumber (slightly thicker than a coin) and add it to your drink. I like to pop three in my Gin & Tonic but feel free to experiment.

### THE WONDERFUL WEDGE *(Fig. 2)*

Simply take your knife and cut a slice of cucumber approximately two fingers in thickness. Slice in half diagonally for a solidly chunky wedge that can sit proudly on top of the long, refreshing Hendrick's drink of your choice.

### THE TANTALISING TONGUE *(Fig. 3)*

Using a vegetable peeler, shave a long, thin length of cucumber to create something that looks like a tongue. You can then curl it around the inside of your glass or gather it like a ribbon and pin it with a cocktail stick, as your creative inclinations direct you.

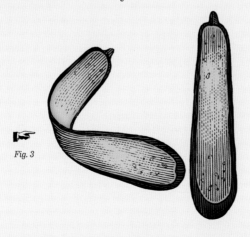

*Fig. 3*

## THE TRUSTY SPEAR  *(Fig. 4)*

———

Tall, green and handsome, the best cucumber spear is cut all the way from the very end of the fruit to capture the gently rounded tip. This is a secret weapon in any drink and can moonlight as an edible stirrer.

## CURIOUS CUCUMBER BALLS  *(Fig. 5)*

———

A melon baller can make beautiful little pale green cucumber balls. Let them roam free in a Hendrick's Gin & Tonic or pin three together with a cocktail stick for an alternative take on a classic Martini garnish.

## ONE CONNECTED CUCUMBER  *(Fig. 6)*

———

Cut two round slices of cucumber and cut a slit towards the middle in each one. Slide each slice into the other at the slit until their fleshy parts connect. If you cut thick slices, this peculiar cucumber garnish will sit short and proud in a Martini glass.

## THE BELOVED BASKET  *(Fig. 7)*

———

Take a thin cucumber slice and pierce one side with a cocktail stick. Thread the cocktail stick through a cucumber ball (prepared with your melon baller), then gently curve the slice around the ball and continue piercing all the way through to the other side.

## THE ROSE  *(Fig. 8)*

———

Take a 5-cm-long round section of cucumber and peel it around its circumference, working from one end to the other to finish with one long peel. Then, starting at the narrower end of the peel, roll it up and style it in a way that makes it look like a rose.

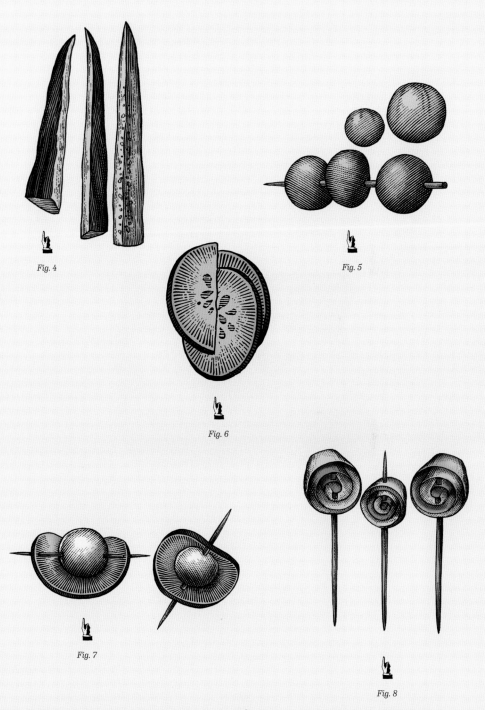

Fig. 4

Fig. 5

Fig. 6

Fig. 7

Fig. 8

# Grow your own
# Gin Palace

FOR THIS CHAPTER it feels only fair that I hand over the reins to the inimitable Lesley Gracie, the master distiller and creator behind everything we do at Hendrick's Gin.

Lesley has always had a fascination with the world of plants and botanicals and she's completely crazy about flowers. Whenever she is in our Gin Palace, you'll find her tending to the plants in the greenhouse, chatting with the gardeners or admiring the wildflowers on the lawns outside.

*Over to you, Lesley...*

The most important thing with gardening is you really have to put plants where they are going to be happy. Plants, like people, thrive when they are in the conditions that suit them best. So if you take a plant that loves to grow free outside and put it inside a hot greenhouse, it won't do so well. Likewise, if you put a plant that loves the sun in a dark, cold room, it won't be happy either. It's about knowing the ideal conditions for each particular plant.

Here are a few suggestions for what you could grow at home, to add a little taste of the Hendrick's Gin Palace experience to your cocktails.

## ROSE

One half of Hendrick's signature flavour duo is rose. We use the oil of precious rose petals and cucumber essence to add a distinctive fragrance to our gin so it transports you back to refreshing summer garden parties with every sip.

Roses are usually quite happy anywhere outside where they have a lot of sun – think 6–8 hours a day – but be guided by the plant, as some like full-on sunshine while others only like partial sun.

Pruning roses is one way to keep them healthy and encourage more beautiful blooms, and cutting back the plant keeps it the size and shape that you want. Pruning can also be quite therapeutic once you get into it.

## CUCUMBER

———

The saying is to be 'cool as a cucumber', because cucumbers are so refreshing. But cucumbers actually don't like to be cool, they like things to be a little warmer. I grow mine at home in a greenhouse, but a sunny spot inside near a window also works.

Cucumbers are relatively easy to grow. Just use a good-quality compost and feed. Because they are an upright plant, you have to grow them up something – so train the plant up a stake or something similar.

Cucumbers are over 95% water, so it stands to reason they like plenty to drink. I water ours a little every day, but I don't leave them sitting in water because that will make them cold and rot the roots.

Cucumbers are the perfect garnish for almost any Hendrick's Gin cocktail, from a classic Hendrick's & Tonic to a Martini.

## ELDERFLOWER

———

I love elderflower. It's one of eleven dried botanicals in Hendrick's Gin. It can be grown at home in the garden and as it grows wild, it'll do its own thing, so you don't need to do anything too drastic with it – just take the flowers when you want.

## CITRUS PLANTS

Citrus, like lemon and lime, adds a light, bright element to a gin or gin cocktail. It's fitting, then, that they like light, bright conditions.

Citrus trees are great things to grow at home. They look great when in blossom and the fruit will provide a natural supply of fresh zing for your cocktails or cooking.

Because citrus trees like a lot of light and warmth, you'll need to put them somewhere nice and bright. Just be sure to shelter them a little from the direct sun or the leaves will start to bake on one side and turn brown. If you don't have a greenhouse, a light, bright spot in the house can work.

## FRESH HERBS

What I like to call windowsill collections, herbs such as basil, thyme, mint and sage are great to grow at home for cooking or cocktails.

You can easily pick up these plants in a local supermarket and they always add a fresh, bright, green element to whatever you're making. They are easy enough to grow, just make sure they are watered regularly. Pull the leaves whenever you want to get a really nice flavour and fragrance for your serves.

# INDEX

Note: page numbers in **bold** refer to illustrations.

I've had the pleasure of working with the world's finest bartenders over the years and I'd like to thank all those who have graciously contributed their imaginative creations to this book and apologise to those I couldn't fit into this one tome.

To my wonderful bunch of Hendrick's brand ambassadors for their support and assistance collating this collection of curious cocktails – thank you.

Huge thanks also go to the creative genius of Lesley Gracie, the OG Hendrick's master distiller and her team of stillmen, Ian Linden, Kevin Gillilan, Gary McNeill and Steven McNeill who work tirelessly to ensure every lovely little batch of Hendrick's Gin is made exactly like the very first.

Thank you to my good pal Celine Weldon, Global Brand Manager at Hendrick's Gin, for all her support getting this project across the line and to everyone who has worked on the brand past and present to help make it what it is.

To Elizabeth Bond, Publishing Director, Ebury Partnerships at Penguin Random House for her belief in this fledgling idea of a book and her hard work in making it a reality.

To Max and Liz Haarala Hamilton for their stunning cocktail photography and styling and to the team at Blairquhan Castle for lending us their incredible backdrop.

Thank you to Sarah Belizaire and the team at BB COMMS for their work behind the scenes bringing this book together.

And last, but certainly not least, thank you to my partner-in-crime, my wonderful wife, Rachel Scott-Martin, who is my favourite martini-drinking companion and who always supports my gin-inspired shenanigans and general tomfoolery.

*Ally Martin, Hendrick's Gin Global Ambassador, travels the world educating and inspiring curious drinkers on the intricate qualities, unique history and heritage of Hendrick's Gin.*

*Originally from Edinburgh, Ally is the ideal envoy for one of Scotland's most celebrated gins and totes the signature rose and cucumber infusion from its home in Girvan, Ayrshire, to share with cocktail connoisseurs near and far. He is an award-winning gin specialist and was shortlisted for Best International Brand Ambassador at Tales of the Cocktail 2022 Spirited Awards in New Orleans.*

*Ally Martin and Lesley Gracie.*

Library of Congress Control Number:
2023947610

ISBN: 978-1-4197-7470-6
eISBN: 979-8-88707-325-5

Text copyright © 2024 Ebury Press
Design copyright © 2024 Ebury Press
Photography copyright © 2024 Ebury Press
Cover © 2024 Ebury Press

Photography: Haarala Hamilton
Photography pages 21, 24, 254: Hendrick's
Drinks Stylist: Tom Woodward
Prop Stylist: Hannah Wilkinson
Design: Sandra Zellmer with Kasia Roy

Ally Martin has asserted his right to be
identified as the author of this Work in
accordance with the Copyright, Designs
and Patents Act 1988

First published in the UK by
Ebury Press in 2023

Published in 2024 by Abrams Image,
an imprint of ABRAMS. All rights reserved.
No portion of this book may be reproduced,
stored in a retrieval system, or transmitted
in any form or by any means, mechanical,
electronic, photocopying, recording, or
otherwise, without written permission from
the publisher.

Printed and bound in China
10 9 8 7 6 5 4 3 2 1

This book features recipes that include the
optional use of raw eggs. Consuming raw eggs
may increase the risk of food-borne illness.
Individuals who are immunocompromised,
pregnant, or elderly should use caution. Ensure
eggs are fresh and meet local food-standard
requirements.

Abrams Image books are available at special
discounts when purchased in quantity
for premiums and promotions as well as
fundraising or educational use. Special editions
can also be created to specification. For details,
contact specialsales@abramsbooks.com or the
address below.

Abrams Image® is a registered trademark of
Harry N. Abrams, Inc.

**ABRAMS** The Art of Books
195 Broadway, New York, NY 10007
abramsbooks.com